TIPS:

Techniques, Ideas, Possibilities and Solutions for Leaders

JOYCE A. FRIEL, MSM, SPHR

DEDICATION

To the mentors in my life…

My father for always believing in me and engraining a belief in myself; he was ever smiling as my wings and my velvet rock.

My husband for allowing me autonomy, independence, and for his unwavering love.

My son for far surpassing all my dreams.

My daughter-in-law for always demonstrating perseverance.

My granddaughter for keeping my dreams alive.

My clients who place their trust in me and my ability to help them optimize their individual and organizational capability and whom I learn from daily.

Being a breakthrough pathfinder is an incurable disease. Only rarely and for brief moments (and always late in the pathfinder's perception) will the pack be with you and reward you for your efforts. The rest of the time, the journey had best be its own reward. Like clapping under water, it is laudable, not audible.

– Dr. Christian Amoroso, who stretched my capability and broadened my horizons.

Contents

TABLE OF CONTENTS

ACKNOWLEDGMENTS

For several years, clients have told me I should write a book – they believe I have something of value to say even when I doubt myself. And for an equally long time I told them I didn't want to use my time in this manner.

Being true to myself, I have to confess that to some degree, I truly didn't want to spend my time writing a book. My husband, Joe Friel, has written several books. I've seen the tremendous effort he expends and I just didn't want to go there. Also I had self-doubt if I really had anything worthy of committing to paper. So why did I decide to launch into this effort when I had so ardently said I wouldn't?

Because as I reviewed the TIPS I'd written over a 10-year span, I realized I wanted to leave a legacy, that I had ideas I wanted to share more broadly than just to those on my distribution list, and that I did have something of value to share. So thank you to my professional colleagues and clients who were persistent. I hope you continue to find value in the TIPS provided in this book.

Table of Contents

POSSIBILITIES

SOLUTIONS

Subject Matter Table of Contents

LEADERSHIP

MANAGEMENT

STRATEGY THINKING/STRATEGIC PLANNING

TEAMWORK

CHAPTER 1
Techniques

Be a Partner for Success

No one is an island. Success comes through working with others toward a common goal. These are truisms you have heard many times before, I'm sure. We have daily reminders of this any time we watch or attend an athletic or artistic performance. Not one of those star performers could be in the spot light or even be selected for the competition if it weren't for the success of the team and each individual's ability to sacrifice their own personal glory for the overall team success. No matter what event you follow this is a true statement even if on the surface it looks like it is a solo performance.

The same is true in business. No business and no leader of any business is successful without a cohesive, well informed, supportive team of individuals who understand where they are going and the role they each play in delivering their collective goal. Each of us needs to know our role, the areas in which we excel and our areas of weakness in order to form a bond and effective partnership with others in our organization.

Right now more than ever, leaders in every part of the organization need to partner with other leaders in their organizations to think differently, strategize to survive and thrive, and address effectively the tough issues all organizations are facing. So what does it mean to be a strategic partner?

Among other things it means:

- Make decisions as if you owned the company – what would you do if the company were your own personal asset and liability? Even when you are an employee, your thinking needs to be entrepreneurial.

- Look ahead for solutions to looming problems before they occur and offer solutions to the leadership team.

- Be willing to deal with the tough choices in a professional, objective, non-partisan manner.

- Remain above the gossip and water cooler talk that often occur in tough times, while being aware of what is being said among the troops.

- Support corporate decisions even if you personally would have made a different choice.

- Stay positive and avoid getting caught up in the negative energy that easily swirls around in tough times.

- Honestly answer these kinds of questions: What value am I delivering? Am I leading restructuring efforts with strategic goals in mind? Have I put metrics in place that truly measure value and contribution? Am I focused on positive contributions and results? Am I keeping my own projects on target and under budget? Am I the living example of what is needed in my organization? Am I providing a confidential ear to other leaders? Am I offering different, creative, effective solutions?
- And, I'm sure you can think of many more examples.

The bottom line is no one will be asked to be at the table or respected for their contributions if they aren't proactive, looking ahead for problems and solutions, making wise financial and human capital decisions, and supporting their fellow employees and leaders. The adage of "we're all in this together" is very appropriate for our current times.

I counsel leaders daily and find the bottom line in most situations is, "Are you doing the right thing, for the right reasons, right now?" If you are, then regardless of how the situation turns out, hold your head high, go home with a clear conscious knowing you did all you could do and you did it well, and then be willing to tackle new issues the next day. If you do, you'll be welcomed as a partner in success and success will come your way.

My Story

At one point in my career I was vying for a position as the Human Resource Manager for one of our company's divisions. The other candidate for the position was a male, he was senior to me in both age and years of service and the company was a male-dominated organization. So I didn't think I was in a lead position although I didn't know for sure. Well, I got the job. When I asked the Division General Manager why he selected me over my colleague, he said it was because he knew I was an entrepreneur. My husband and I owned a retail store so he knew I had experience managing the bottom line while I also had to focus on growing the top line.

Every employee needs to bring that entrepreneurial spirit to work with them. Whether we own the assets and carry the liabilities of the firm directly or not is irrelevant. We all need to act "as if" the company is our own. We'll all make better decisions if we approach our work with this mindset.

Brain Storming and Brain Writing

I'm sure you have noticed as have I that the world seems to get smaller all the time. I realized this was true recently on a trip to Bangkok. In the Bangkok airport, I picked up a great business magazine call *Extraordinary Lives*. One of the articles in the magazine was called "Brain Storming: The Good, the Bad and the Ugly" by Dr. Detlef Reis from Mahidol University in Bangkok.

Brain storming has been around since 1953 when it was first introduced by Alex Osborn in his *Applied Imagination* book. The article provides very useful tips for making these types of creative sessions more productive. Brain storming is a frequently used tool. If you do a Google search on the word you'll get over 11 million responses versus 1.5 million when you search on creativity techniques.

The down side of using a familiar tool such as brain storming is that many people think they know how to do it, yet few conduct such sessions well so less than optimal results are generated. The upside is most of what is done incorrectly is very easy to remedy.

Ideas for improved brain storming:

- Assign a facilitator to run the session and a recorder to capture the ideas.

- Defer judgment until the end of the session – don't kill the idea by debating it during the idea generation phase.

- Go for quantity – the more the better. The more ideas you get the greater probability some of them will be winners.

- The more outside the box, the wilder, the crazier the better – some will be real gems.

- Combine ideas that have been submitted, improve on the ideas of others.

- Recognize that even at it's best brainstorming is inferior to brain writing.

- Improved idea generation through brain writing:

    o Write down ideas individually and independently. Then share them – this generates approximately 4 times as many ideas than the same size group can generate while brain storming. Write them on index cards or Post-It notes.

    o Better results are generated because everyone participates – no one is freeloading.

    o There is less reluctance to submit creative ideas because brain writing is done anonymously rather than verbally.

    o Ideas are not blocked by waiting for one person to finish speaking before the next idea can be contributed.

    o Everyone is doing their own thinking simultaneously and, as a result, more ideas get generated and time is utilized more effectively.

Best of both:

- Review the rules of brain storming and brain writing before you begin.

- Have a facilitator and a recorder available. Allow and encourage the facilitator to interject other creativity generating techniques into the process to continue stimulation and keep the energy levels high.

- To get the best of both techniques, hold a brain writing session prior to brain storming. It's easy. Each person has a pen and 3x5 index cards or Post-It notes. All participants simultaneously write one idea per card. Continue until idea generation slows. Read each idea aloud and cluster the ideas by topic. Then open up the session to brain storming and get out of the way as tons of ideas flow.

Following these simple guidelines will make your creative sessions more effective, energizing and productive.

My Story

The first time I encountered brain writing I was working with a colleague designing a workshop where a group of employees were going to be split off from a traditional work environment into a self-managed team structure. There was a lot of trepidation and uncertainty as the concept of self-managed teams was new, it certainly was a first for this organization, and "the jury was out" regarding the success of the venture. It was critical to get at the heart of what people were thinking and respect their feelings. As designers we felt brain storming would prevent people from sharing their true feelings and yet knowing what they really felt was critical. So we used the brain writing technique. It worked!

Quickly, easily and without putting anyone on the spot we were able to identify feelings and concerns. Because we could get at the heart of the matter in a safe, respectful way, people were willing to engage in an open dialog about solutions. Consider it when you are faced with a similar dilemma.

Check √ the Boxes

So often we get caught up in focusing on the bottom line: What the P&L statement says, what Wall Street demands, what the shareholders want, what the manager requires, how we're doing against this month's goals, meeting quotas, etc. As a society we are conditioned to focus on the results rather than the process so it is no wonder we end up with head aches, tight muscles in our neck and shoulders, ulcers and premature aging. I have no doubt that this all sounds much too familiar.

However, there is another perspective that I find relieves some of the tension and often produces better results. What more could an entrepreneurial society like ours want than less tension and better results?

I recently had the great fortune to meet and speak with Lisa Norden, World Champion Sprint Distance triathlete and her coach Darren Smith. Lisa is from Sweden and Darren is from Australia and they were in Davos, Switzerland for a race season training camp. The world of elite, professional triathlon is extremely competitive and grueling. Lisa was asked the question, "How do you manage to stay focused and not get discouraged by the pain, grueling distances and overwhelming pressure". She replied that she races by checking the boxes and the results take care of themselves.

I have always been a believer that focusing on the process is the key to getting improved results so I was all ears about her concept of "checking the boxes". Lisa doesn't focus on the goal of winning the race, she focuses on the goal of getting each of the individual actions executed with precision and excellence. She mentally checks each box and the World Championship results take care of themselves.

Did I do everything in my preparation stage?　√

When I set up my transition, was everything in its proper place and order? √

When I entered the water, did I get the surge I needed in that first 200 meters? √

Was I in the right position at the first buoy in the water? √

When I exited the swim to my bike, was I focused and racing my own pace regardless of what other competitors were doing? √

Did I stay within my power zones without getting distracted by others? √

If there were uncontrollable obstacles like head winds, rain or rough roads, did I turn these into positive challenges rather than cursing my bad luck? √

Lisa knows the podium finish on the top step will be assured if she manages each process step along the way with excellence. Stress is relieved by focusing on small steps rather than the overall daunting task, energy and excitement are built as you experience how well you are successfully managing the parts of the whole, and confidence builds as you celebrate completion along the way.

Lisa's technique serves as a good example for all of us in business, also. Rather than focusing on the year-end goals, the competitive pressures, and the external demands which often seem overwhelming, if we choose to focus on all the controllable aspects throughout the process we will be assured the desired results will occur.

No one sells a bottom line, no one manufactures a net profit, no one produces an exponential improvement as a product per se. What we all do regardless of our business or service is manage the myriad of process steps along the way to produce and sell our products or services. Just like Lisa, we can produce hugely improved results with less stress and tension if we focus on checking the boxes along the way rather than the daunting overall goal.

So what is your goal? What is required to produce the results you need to achieve? What are the sequential steps necessary? Do you completely understand the goal and it's importance to your organization? If not, this is step No. 1. Have you done your preparation and training to build your capability? If not, this is step No 2. Can you put a √ there? If you are prepared, then check the boxes as you produce, service or manufacture.

Build your checklist based on values and principles. Integrity (you can't check the box if you didn't perform the task with accuracy and excellence), tenacity (only check the box if each step was complete and correct), and quality (place a check mark if your work product represents your brand and your customers will be delighted with it) are a few of the values upon which your checklist must be built. Build in the right values, diligently use the checklist and your seemingly overwhelming goals will be met and frequently exceeded.

Just imagine the power that comes from getting your whole organization checking the boxes and focusing on doing their best, one step at a time. Just like Lisa, you'll be World Champions, achieve your goals, and have less stress along the way.

My Story

A funny thing happened in the grocery store one day. I was clipping right along grabbing as I went zipping down the aisles. I was a woman on a mission. I buzzed around the corner and there was a colleague of mine from work. He was an electrical engineer and I knew from his Myers-Briggs Type* that he was the kind of person who liked to wing it when it came to non-technical tasks, he just couldn't be bothered with process unless it was job-related. Yet, there he was standing right in front of the dairy case with his Day Timer and pencil checking off his list.

I said "Eric, what are you doing? You're using a list. That's not like you at all." He replied, "Well, I'm a single Dad and the kids are with me this weekend and I've found if I don't use a list, I forget their favorite things and, of course, I also get home without the essentials so I've learned to use a list".

"So you're back to using a process to get the job done just like at work, huh," I said.

"Yep, it works. It helps me get the job done faster and more completely", he replied.

So even with mundane tasks like the groceries, process is often the key to reducing stress and improving results.

*The Myers-Briggs Type Indicator instrument and the MBTI are registered trademarks of Consulting Phychologists Press, Inc.

Client's Lessons from Using Balanced Scorecard Strategic Planning

A group of fellow female business owners and I hold an annual retreat to develop our respective business strategies. We call ourselves the MM's which is short for Master Minds. We use a Balanced Scorecard (BSC) approach in developing our business strategies. A Balanced Scorecard ensures a balanced focus on the financial, stakeholder, process improvement and human aspects necessary to create, manage and produce balanced results. For more details, reference the work of Robert Kaplan and David Norton who are often published in Harvard Business Review articles and have published books on the BSC methodology.

As a good practice we always start by not only scoring and sharing our results to-date, but also reflecting on the lessons learned about ourselves, our businesses, and the process of using a Balanced Scorecard strategy. I want to share our recent reflections with you as I suspect some of these are identical to your own experiences and some may be lessons you will yet discover.

Those of you who have worked with me to develop your strategic plans know that I give you several cautions when we start out. For example, even with good consulting and discussion along the way you will have a tendency to put more major improvement opportunities in your plan than you can realistically manage in a year's time. Also, it will take about 3 years of experience and self-discovery to know what the best measures are for the initiatives you are working on. Nonetheless, the progress you make and the focus you gain along the way will help you achieve greater results than you otherwise could have attained. With these caveats in mind, the following are the key insights we have discovered. I hope they help you in your business planning. These are quotes from various Master Mind members.

- Using the Balanced Scorecard is an amazing tool for creating and staying focused. Because we are focused on the critical few initiatives needed to move our businesses forward, we are achieving results we couldn't have realized otherwise.

- We're busting a myth that says you can't make money in some industries in your own back yard. We are living proof this is not true since revenues are up 140% over last year and a very large portion of that income is in our own metro area.

- Because we use our time more wisely by focusing on the critical few initiatives driving our businesses, we now have time to devote to giving back to our community and gaining a life balance we didn't have before.

- Scoring, charting and sharing our results validates that we are worth what other's tell us we are worth and it validates the worthiness of what we do. Seeing results and achieving stretch goals demonstrates this dramatically and cements it is in our minds both intellectually and emotionally.

- Being small entrepreneurial companies, there is tremendous value from developing our respective strategies with other "solopreneur's". Together we help each other not only validate our plans, but see opportunities and possibilities we alone could not have identified. Validation from others not only causes us to put initiatives in our plans we would not have been able to identify alone, it also gives us the energy and drive to achieve more than we otherwise would accomplish.

- Because of the discipline we get from using the Balanced Scorecard process, we use our time much more profitably and can actually quantify the value of it through our results. We are each in a much richer, more rewarding, more balanced place than we would have been able to achieve without the focus, discipline and accountability we have gained by using this process.

What better way to build your business than to reflect on the learning you have gained from your business this past year and incorporate that insight into where you want to take your business and how you will get there in the future. We've been meeting monthly for our accountability meetings and annually to create our strategies for seven years now. I have every confidence that we are each more successful and better business owners because of our encouragement, perseverance in using a proven process, and our continual accountability to each other. How might you apply some of what we've learned to help propel your own business forward?

My Story

I stumbled into Kaplan and Norton's work in the early 90's. I had a habit of reading the Harvard Business Review when I traveled as I often did in those days. It was a great way to relax, learn and pass the time at 35,000 over the Midwest.

No one told me to do so, but I decided to take our corporate Balanced Score Card (BSC) and the BSC for the division I supported and for the division I reported to and make my own, personal BSC. It took several iterations at first, but after I had it refined, I reviewed the result with my division general manager and the general manager to whom I reported. Both loved it. It made it easy for them to see what I was doing to drive results, it made it easy to focus on the right things, measuring progress was simple, and best of all, it made reporting my results to them quick and painless. And, of course, anytime you make your bosses job easier they are pleased. While it wasn't necessarily my intent, it also almost guaranteed a raise. How could they not reward a person who was focused on creating results for their division and who continually kept them informed of progress and needs in order to achieve success? Deciding to use a personal BSC was a blessing in disguise from a salary –enhancement perspective, but the greatest reward was knowing I was making a difference and how I was personally contributing to success.

Credit to Carolyn

I'm generally not to keen on sitcom's and reality TV programs. However, once in a while you get caught up and along the way you are not only entertained, but you might learn something. This happened to me several seasons back while watching "The Apprentice".

If you've never watched it, in this series Donald Trump had two of his Executive Vice President's (EVP) accompany him into the Board Room to review team results and determine who would be fired from the group of apprentice applicants each week. One EVP was George Ross. The other was Carolyn Kepcher. Both were impressive, but I wanted to know more about the young, sharp, female EVP and COO. I purchased a book she wrote entitled, *Carolyn 101: Business Lessons from The Apprentice's Straight Shooter*. What a treat this turned out to be. Not only did I get to learn the incredible story of how she ended up working for the Trump Organization, I also learned some new lessons and was reminded of other valuable ones.

Since we are all very busy and reading is one thing we all probably wish we had more time to do, I have a gift for you – the Cliff Notes version of *Carolyn 101*. Here are some great reminders in no particular order.

- Every employee, at every level, is a salesman (or saleswoman).

- Some sort of personal connection has to precede the professional connection. Ultimately, our business success is relationship-oriented.

- Good Employee Rules

    1. If one player wins, we all win, if one player loses, we all lose.

    2. Everybody on our team has to appreciate everyone else's job.

    3. You've got to want to be there.

    4. Be in the know.

    5. Bring a solution, not a problem.

    6. When in doubt, make a decision and stand by it.

    7. Become an expert in your field.

- Bad Employee Rules

    1. Have an unhealthy attitude.

    2. Fail to show up.

    3. Fail to swim when you are dropped into the water.

- When it comes to kids and work, know where to draw the line; your kids always come first.

- Rules for Good Meetings

    1. All meetings are conducted by the One-Minute Rule. I close the door one minute after the meeting was supposed to start, anyone who turns up late misses the meeting.

    2. Always have an agenda.

    3. Address all agenda topics first, then any items needing discussion which are not on the agenda.

    4. Encourage input from all, but never let meetings be dominated by one or two people.

5.   Before speaking, ask yourself these questions:

Does my input truly contribute to our general understanding of the issue or am I just taking up air space?

Am I providing a fresh perspective or could I be undermining the authority of the person to whom I am directing my suggestions?

My Story

Carolyn believes, as do I, that all business ultimately is relationship-based. Some how she managed to develop a relationship with The Donald just prior to or during the interviewing process or he wouldn't have hired her. I'm confident she was following her own set of rules listed above. No wonder she impressed him. These are a good set of rules. Wouldn't you like to hire a manager who espouses and lives these?

Early Warning Signs

Life is full of early warning signs. Unfortunately, we all too often overlook them or ignore them altogether until it is too late. We all know about health indicators which give us warnings, weather forecasters who forewarn danger, and any number of financial indicators that give us warnings; but what warning signs do you have as organizational barometers or warning signals? This article is about the barometers in your organization.

If you answer "No" to any of the questions below, consider these "early warning signs" of potential organizational weaknesses or areas where problems may emerge in the future. Hopefully you are able to respond with a "Yes" to all these statements. If not, don't despair. Select one or two of the items you answered "No" to that are of most importance to your organization and work on closing the gap. Then work on the next one or two until you've made progress. Exceptional organizations focus on doing a 1,000 things 1% better, not doing 1 thing 1,000% better. Best of luck on your self-assessment!

<u>WARNING SIGN</u>

Strategy and Governance

Do you have a written statement of the organization's Vision, Mission and Guiding Principles or Values? Yes or No _____

If you have a Vision, Mission and Guiding Principles or Values statement is it publicized? Yes or No _____

Do you have a strategic plan? Yes or No _____

If you have a strategic plan is it shared with everyone in the organization? Yes or No _____

Do you have stated target goals for this year's critical performance initiatives? Yes or No _____

Do you have metrics which track organizational performance throughout the year against the targeted goals? Yes or No _____

Are the targeted goals and metrics (if you have them) shared with everyone in the organization? Yes or No _____

Are the organization's financial goals integrated with internal processes, customer needs and the development and growth of employees? Yes or No _____

Does the organization have a governance policy which the Board and senior managers must follow? Yes or No _____

Communication

Does everyone in the organization know what they have to do to help the organization reach its goals? Yes or No _____

Does the organization have all-employee meetings or another method of keeping everyone informed of organizational results and progress, as well as, challenges as they come up throughout the year? Yes or No _____

Does the organization tailor the style, method and frequency of communications to the audience and message content? Yes or No _____

If the organization expects mid-managers and supervisors to communicate information to their units is there a communications strategy and method for ensuring the message gets delivered consistently to everyone? Yes or No _____

Does the organization have mechanisms and processes for employees to communicate up the channel? Yes or No _____

In the organization does information flow freely both up and down the channel?   Yes or No _____

Leadership Development and Training

Does each employee receive a performance review at least annually?   Yes or No _____

Does each employee have a personal development plan which is reviewed at least annually with their supervisor?   Yes or No _____

Do employees receive training each year which is specific to their current job or a position they are being prepared for in the future?   Yes or No _____

Does the organization track the results of training so that what is learned gets applied on the job?   Yes or No _____

Does the organization have both supervisory and management training for people in these roles?   Yes or No _____

Does the organization have a succession planning process which identifies key positions and emerging leaders?   Yes or No _____

Do the individuals in the succession plan get specific mentoring, coaching and development in order to be able to step into key roles when needed?   Yes or No _____

Does the organization have a specific methodology they use for leading significant change?   Yes or No _____

Does the organization spend intentional time developing the ability of the senior leadership team to work effectively together?   Yes or No _____

Accountability

Do employees (including managers and supervisors) take responsibility for issues when they come up or is it "someone else's" problem?   Yes or No _____

Does the organization have job expectations and standards for all positions?   Yes or No _____

Are people held accountable for achieving results?   Yes or No _____

Are employees rewarded and recognized for work well done and coached when they fall short?   Yes or No _____

Does the organization proactively eliminate those employees who infect others with negative attitudes and who don't contribute?   Yes or No _____

Do those employees who truly are exemplary get the recognition and rewards they deserve?   Yes or No _____

Certainly the above list is not exhaustive. There are hundreds of things that can be warning signs of impending peril. However, if you were able to honestly answer "Yes" to the vast majority of these statements, you are well out of harms way and likely doing much better than your competition. Congratulations! If you had a lot of "No" responses, determine the one or two items that are most important to your organization? What actions are you going to take very soon to eliminate these potential dangers? Monitoring the barometer of your organization is the best way to avoid employee, leadership and organizational performance problems in the future.

My Story

What I have listed above is my mental cheat sheet for sizing up an organization. I can quickly find out a lot of this information. I know what some of their significant performance gaps are and I know where they excel. As a result, I know what I'm up against, whether or not I even want to work with the client and, I know what depth and breadth of work I will need to do. It took me a few years of experience to develop the list and pinpoint the issues, but you have years of experience in your own field.

Develop your own similar set of questions to use as a mental guide for sizing up your clients, prospects, employees, etc. The more you have a mental check list readily in mind the quicker you can get focused solving problems and meeting expectations.

Getting Results from Group Meetings

While having a professional facilitator allows you to fully participate while the facilitator focuses on the meeting process, there are times when you just don't have this luxury. Here are a few key ideas that will help you be prepared, use your time wisely, and achieve the results you want.

<u>Purpose</u> – What is the purpose of the gathering or meeting. Be able to succinctly and concisely state the purpose and outcomes you want to achieve. Knowing the purpose is your guide to effective utilization of time and achieving results. Are you focusing on sales, marketing, clients, process improvement, problem solving, making a specific decision, recognition, or motivation? Each of these topics has different requirements in order to achieve results.

<u>ROI</u> – List specific ROI results you want based upon the purpose statement. You should be able to state either a hard dollar or a soft dollar result this gathering or meeting is intended to achieve. You need to be able to answer the questions, "What do I want the attendees to do as a result of being here"? "What do I want the outcome of this meeting to be"?

<u>Environment</u> – The mind can only remember what the seat can absorb so your goal is to create the environment, format and flow that allows a timely, productive process.

<u>If The Shoe Fits</u> - I credit Don Woodward, Technical Director for Sonshine Enterprises, with this analogy. If I asked you how much a pair of shoes costs, you would immediately ask more questions. What will you use the shoes for? How much are you willing to pay for them? What kind of shoes do you want? You need to approach planning your gathering from the same perspective. In this case, the form truly does follow the function. What do you want to achieve dictates how you design the gathering.

<u>Rehearse</u> – Mentally or verbally conduct a quick walkthrough. How will you open the event? What are the points you'll summarize in the closing? How will you handle any anticipated rough spots? What specific comments will be made to ensure the points you want discussed get addressed? Visualize yourself conducting the session to get the desired results. As the designer/facilitator, your role is to make sure the overall event exceeds the sum of the separate parts.

Keeping these few quick guides in mind will help you as a business owner and manager, prepare for and get the ROI you want from the meetings you conduct.

My Story

Any time I contract to facilitate a work session, I start with the end in mind. Of course, this concept was popularized by Dr. Stephen Covey and while I didn't know to call it that…starting with the end in mind…I did it long before I read Covey's work.

How as a consultant could I possibly understand my client's expectations without knowing what their end game was? I have to know what they desire as an end product before I begin. We don't always end up there because I often find my clients can describe the symptoms, but don't know how to identify the root causes. While I have to understand their "end in mind" expectations, I often counsel them to produce a different product with a process more appropriate to solving their underlying problems. After all, that is what they hired me for. If they knew how to identify the root cause and how to fix the problem, they wouldn't need me.

So one of the first questions I ask is what are the expected deliverables as a result of this work? What do they have as the "end in mind"? Ask these questions of yourself as you design your own group work processes and you'll either end up with a better process or you may find your "end in mind" expectations need to change.

Key Components of a Strategic Plan

You all know the saying that any road will do as long as you don't know where you are going. And it is certainly true when it comes to achieving company goals. If you don't have stated goals, have them written down, well communicated, and measured, there is a very high probability you'll never achieve them. Thus, the importance of having a quantifiable, measurable strategic plan.

Roadmap

Strategic planning is like creating a map for an exciting journey. A map helps keep you on course, but it isn't so stringent that you can't check out a side road along the way. Each year in the fall I map out where I am against my company goals, where I want to go, and how I want to get there. During the year, my plan then becomes my guide as I make business decisions and come upon new opportunities. It helps me decide if new opportunities and the choices I encounter will get me closer to my goals or if detours are to be avoided. It is critical to at least annually review your plan to accommodate new developments in technology, client requests, the economy, emerging trends, and your own interests.

Key Components

Below are the key components and a diagram of the flow for creating a Strategic Business Plan.

1. SWOT - The first step is to determine where you are by doing a SWOT analysis. Identify your internal Strengths and Weaknesses and your external Opportunities and Threats. Make a grid and fill in the blanks. Use two columns and two sections. Section headings are for internal and external and the columns are for strengths and weaknesses; and opportunities and threats. Then brainstorm to fill in the chart. Internally analyze human, financial, technological resources, culture, etc. Externally examine the economy, political/regulatory, social/demographic, technology, competition, etc. Ask your key contributors to do this same exercise. It is also wise to get a valued opinion from someone external to your organization.

2. Vision and Mission – Craft a short statement that quickly and easily describes your purpose (Mission) and your ultimate future (Vision). Again it is helpful to brainstorm. Who are your clients/customers, what makes you different, how would your customers describe you, what do you offer, how are you unique, what do you want your company to be like tomorrow? Here is a quick template to follow: "The purpose of ABC Company is to _(what do you do?)_____ so that the company and your stakeholders benefit from __(what are your products or services?)_____resulting in ___(what will be the results when you do what this statement says you will do?)_____. This quickly states who you are, why you exist, and what benefits occur as a result of your business. You can get clever later on, but for now simply get this statement on paper.

3. Objectives – Identify the key objectives that have to be met in order to achieve your vision and mission. State them in specific, quantifiable, measurable terms. They need to be ambitious, but realistic. Focus on "what, not how". Your list will grow, but pare it down to the critical 4-5 most important items for advancing your business in the next 12 months.

4. Action Planning - Now we'll look at the "how". For each objective you listed in step 3, create a detailed action plan of how you will meet this goal. For each objective state:

   ✓ Desired results – what will happen or what benefit will occur; make your statement quantifiable?
   ✓ Potential obstacles/barriers – what might stand in your way or prevent progress?
   ✓ Support – what resources, people, tools do you have or need?

5. Implementation Process – What steps must be taken – indicate who will do what and by when.

6. Evaluation and Measurement - How will you know you've successfully achieved the objectives (this is why each must be stated so it is specific, quantifiable and measurable)? As you get more sophisticated, a set of balanced scorecard measures is an ideal way to track, measure, and communicate your progress, but for now just determine how each objective will be measured.

I do a monthly review to see what is on target, what is falling behind, what follow-up is needed, etc. This gives me a visual update and reminds me of my targets and how I am progressing.

This seems like a lot of work, but if you'll map out each objective you will have a clear picture of where you're going, how to get there, and achieve your goals quicker since you'll avoid unnecessary, costly detours.

For those of you who learn better through pictures than words, here is a graphic of the process.

Strategic Planning Process and Framework

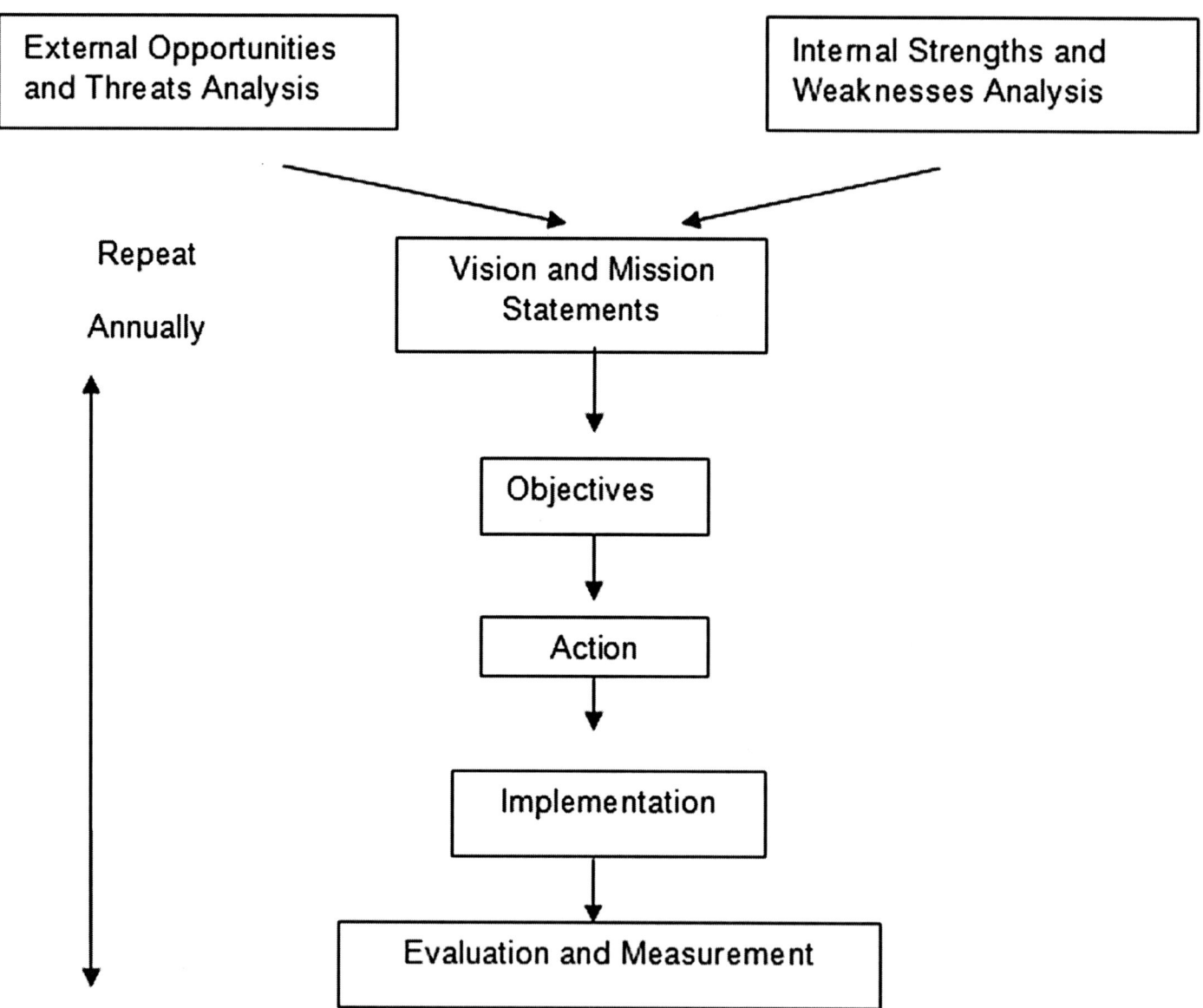

The simplicity of these steps and descriptions belie the difficulty of this task. I have facilitated many senior management teams that struggle getting even the first two steps done. However, if you set aside quiet time with your key colleagues and valued advisors, this need not be a monumental task. Once you have it in place, the annual process of reviewing, revising and refreshing becomes not only much easier, but very beneficial. You walk away from this exercise with a sense of direction and satisfaction about how you are going to achieve your business goals with the assurance of avoiding at least some unnecessary, costly detours.

My Story

I wrote this particular TIPS article for two reasons. One, everyone wants a quick fix. So I've given you the Cliff Notes version of how to construct and work your way through a strategic plan. It appears to be quick and easy on paper, but to do a quality job and really get at the heart of issues that will present themselves as obstacles later on, it takes honest, open dialog and time.

Secondly, I put the chart in the article because I know about 50% of the population likes to see things in writing and the other 50% likes pictures. So no matter how your mind works, you've got a quick road map for creating a strategic plan.

I often use a similar set of documents as a template to help clients understand the various process steps we will be going through as a part of the journey toward creating their organizational strategic plan. I find they like to see where we are and how much we have to do yet and they like to know which steps we've completed and what comes next both visually on the chart and as a checklist in the process steps. It is necessary to do both so everyone is on the same page no matter how their mind works.

Leading Change Successfully

To stay competitive there is no other option than to continually strive to become more efficient, effective, and precise in what you do and how you do it. From the customer's perspective it is expected, from the owner's perspective it is required, but from the leader and employee's perspective achieving improvement is often confusing.

Leading change is a management function. It must be intentionally planned and lead. It cannot be left to chance. If you are looking for a quick fix, launching a change effort is not the answer.

So what do you do, how do you get started, and do you even want to go there? Let's assume you do "want to go there". Even if you are already the very best, you won't stay at the top for very long if you rest on your laurels so welcome to life as a "change leader".

OK, so now that I'm a change leader, what do I do? What do I do differently than I'm doing now? While there are volumes written giving the details of how change has played out both successfully and unsuccessfully in many companies, underlying many of these stories are a few key principles. While there are no guarantees, these fundamentals can be found as core elements in almost every successful change effort. These will not guarantee success, but the absence of these critical ingredients is very likely to cause failure.

<u>Key to Success</u> - The key to successful improvement and change efforts is leveraging human potential. How many times have you heard, "Just tell me what to do and I'll do it". When I hear this phrase I don't think of employees just waiting to be told what to do. I hear a cry for direction. As an employee I needed to know what to change and why - and your followers need to know this too?

A recent Harris pole found that only 37% of those polled had a clear understanding of what the organization was trying to achieve and only 20% were enthusiastic about their organization's goals. If only a minor percentage of your followers know what is expected you have a very weak probability of achieving your goals. So the first step in leveraging human potential and leading change effectively is to clearly define and communicate what needs to change and why. What is the urgency, what is the impetus driving the change, what adverse consequences will happen if the change doesn't occur, why is the improvement or change critical to your business success? How does this change fit into the overall strategic direction you are trying to take the company? And most important of all, what is in it for the employees? Why should they care about getting behind the effort? Employees have to understand why the company is dissatisfied with the present situation and how it will affect them before they can rally their energy to join the effort.

<u>Change to What</u> – What is the vision, literally a descriptive picture, of what the organization is trying to achieve? You won't leverage human potential and get employees engaged in the change effort if they don't understand both why and what the "future state" is supposed to look like. Visit another company that has already accomplished what you want, use videos to demonstrate, pilot a project to show them results, spend time talking in small groups about the current situation and what the future will be like once the change is achieved. You first have to know why to change and then you have to know what to change to before committed actions can take place.

<u>WIIFM</u> – So what's in it for me (WIIFM)? What incentive is there for employees to change and for leaders to step up to the challenge? I am not one who believes change is particularly difficult. Change is much easier when you understand the imperative and benefit you will receive from making the change. The difficult part comes when the change may be beneficial, in fact, absolutely necessary for the company, but it doesn't appear to have many immediate benefits for the employees. In these situations, you have to find win/win scenarios and very intentionally recruit peer leaders and influential employees to help sway the opinions of the majority. Ultimately, if it benefits the company it will benefit the employees, but as a leader you are responsible for helping employees see the connection and ultimate benefit.

<u>Getting Started</u> - Assess the situation and plan for success. What factors will aid success and what challenges will you face? Recruit influential peers to serve as group leaders and together build a "Plan for Change". Among other things it should include an explanation of the need for change, a list of the key leaders and influencers and the naysayers you'll need to influence, a description of what success will look like, a list of obstacles and a plan to remove or overcome them. Start small, celebrate early

successes and celebrate genuine improvement and success often, and praise those making the change happen. Leverage small wins into bigger ones.

Sustaining Gains - In two words – Liberally Communicate! You cannot over-communicate. When you think you've said it all, say it again in a different way and keep doing it. Change, even if it is welcomed, is emotional and when your emotions are involved it is more difficult to hear the rationale for change. A key component of your "Plan for Change" is your communications plan. The more emotional the content and the more complex the message to the recipients the more you have to communicate. Increase the frequency, vary the method, provide time to dialog and discuss, and then do it again.

Creating the Change Culture – The culture of your organization is a by-product of the processes, policies, practices and procedures which guide and mold the behavior of the people. As progress is made you have to assess and modify where needed the company processes, policies and procedures to support not only the change effort, but also to reinforce and support the gains. You will get early wins and these are the stepping stones to bigger and more significant improvements, but to truly institute an improvement culture where employees embrace and lead change at every level is a long-term affair requiring constant review, planning, and leadership. In the best organizations, the Human Resources and Organizational Development staff are involved early on in understanding the business rationale, formulating the plans, and continually supporting the leaders, employees and company structures needed to transform the culture.

Summary - One manager I spoke with very recently told me they have the "Rule of 2 Kings" in their company. One king is the customer and the other king is the employees. Leaders of change would do well to adopt this rule because serving the first king is why the improvement change effort is necessary and serving the second king is how you go about achieving the cultural transformation.

My Story

What I've provided above is a simplified version of John Kotter's change management principles mixed in with my own experiences. I am mentoring a Human Resource Manager for a large global mining firm. He knows as his organization evolves and as he advances he needs to know more about Organizational Development to complement his HR skill set. He is a wise man. HR is tactical for the most part while OD is strategy. Together they make a rich skill set to help facilitate change and leadership development within organizations. We've been working together about 15 months and have a few more months to go. We are using an action research approach so the protégé is directing the topics we cover depending on what his need is at the time. In every case no matter what the topic we're working on there is a large component of change management. So while he is learning to be the change facilitator for his firm, every manager is a change leader in their own right. It is impossible to lead effectively without also being a successful change leader.

Parallels of Golf and Leading Your Business

First of all I want to credit my friend, client and fellow golfer, Deb Waitkus, with the idea for this article. Deb is the founder and CEO of Golf for Cause (www.golfforcause.com). She is an expert in demystifying the game, turning 'Golf into Gold™, and leveraging golf for business.

Her recent newsletter focused on the Rules of Golf which, as you may know, can be very obscure, daunting, and at times bewildering. It struck me as I read them there are many parallels between golf and leading a business. The rules of leading effectively can also be quite daunting and at times bewildering.

The Royal and Ancient Golf Club may not have had business lessons in mind when those rugged Scotsmen devised this challenging game, but they did us all a great service both recreationally and professionally when they codified the rules of the game over the years. Here are a few samples of how golf and business parallel each other.

Golf	Business
Penalty Strokes	OK, you goofed. You did something by mistake or even knowingly did something that you could have done better. Be honest about it, admit the error, take the penalty stroke, learn from the error and move on.
Maximum 14 Clubs	What are the 14 "go to" tools you use most frequently and effectively to lead and manage? Golfers are always buying new clubs to get that edge. They know they can only carry 14 clubs, but they want the clubs that help them achieve their goal most effectively and work diligently to find them. Are your "leadership tools" the ones you need in your bag?
Be Ready	Being prepared and ready for your next shot is critical in maintaining pace of play and enjoying your round of golf. Are you anticipating and are you ready to meet your next business challenge? Are you considering the lie, have you lined up your next move, can you visualize the ability of your company to respond, are the other players on your team ready to respond?
Etiquette	Golf is not just about getting the lowest score. It is also about etiquette, honesty and following the rules. You learn a great deal about a person's character, ethic and personal code of conduct when you play a round of golf with them. Wouldn't it be nice to know how your potential clients and colleagues react under pressure before you engage them in business? You can learn this in a friendly round of golf. Do you include playing golf with clients and colleagues as a key component of your business strategic development?

For those of you that are golfers I have adapted with Deb's permission the Slow Play Test from one of the Golf for Cause newsletter to a **Slow Play Test for Leaders and Managers**.

Slow Play Test for Leaders and Managers	Yes	No
1. Am I courteous?		
2. Am I aware of the needs of others in order to help them succeed?		
3. Do I know when it is appropriate to make the next move to close the deal or coach a subordinate?		
4. Am I ready and proactive when action is needed?		
5. Do I note the reaction and change in market to my strategy and tactics; do I learn from the markets reaction?		
6. Do I delay and procrastinate to avoid difficulty decisions?		
7. If in doubt, do I have a contingency plan prepared?		
8. Am I decisive and committed to my decisions?		
9. Do I know how to "take relief" and guide my team when minor adjustments need to be made?		
10. Am I preparing for my next leadership action as I observe the activities of my team?		
11. Do I note the score, take a quick assessment of results and then move on rather than dwelling on the past?		
12. Do I have the correct 14 clubs in my leadership tool bag to ensure my success as a leader?		

Golf is a wonderful venue for relaxing, enjoying nature, having fun and an extremely useful business skill. If you need to sharpen you leadership skills, now is the time to get to the driving range to tune up your game and close any gaps revealed in the **Short Game Test for Leaders and Managers.**

My Story

It just doesn't get much better than doing business on the golf course. Nature provides such a wonderful backdrop for relaxing and yet really getting to know a person's true character. In one business my husband was involved with he had the practice of not hiring a person until he had played golf with them. You do truly learn a person's character on the golf course. The best and the worst will come out.

I frequently use an instrument called the **Golf Stroke Saver™.** The feedback report is written in terms of behavior on the golf course. For example, if the person is a high D (Driver, Dominant type), they are going to be fast paced, let's get it done kind of person. If they are in a business golf setting, wouldn't it be helpful if they knew the type of their client-playing partner? If this person is also a high D, they will likely rush through the game, forget to stop and appreciate nature around them, and possibly not even focus on identifying, let alone discussing, their business opportunities. Mind you, you don't have to talk business while you are playing, but at least think about when is it appropriate to have this discussion during your outing together possibly at the 19th hole. But if the client is an S (Steady, Social) they may be uncomfortable with fast play. They may want a steady, even-paced play, but because they want to keep harmony they may be very uncomfortable commenting about the pace of play. Now if they are the client and you are the host, you may have just lost the deal and you haven't even talked business yet.

Regardless of your type or the type of your client, mirror their pace and anticipate their needs. This is true on and off the course. Above all enjoy the round and enjoy each other's company because ultimately business is based upon relationships and golf is a wonderful venue for a solid relationship.

The ABC's of Behavior

Culture, as a collective set of beliefs and behaviors, forms the foundation of all organizations. Our beliefs cause us to behave in particular ways and, consequently, also determine the collective results achieved (or not achieved) by organizations. Our attitudes are how we choose to display our values and our values generally don't change without a very significant event occurring. We cannot see values, we only learn of other's values by seeing them displayed through their behaviors. Whew! That was a long series of cause-and-effect statements, but the bottom line of it is that our behaviors make up our culture and, of course, we have choices in our behaviors so we have choices in the cultures we create.

Intellectually this makes sense, but on a practical basis, how do you change behavior? After all, leaders spend a lot of time managing the situations resulting from behaviors, so let's get practical about this topic. This simple Antecedent-Behavior-Consequence (ABC) tool is a quick way to analyze behaviors.

Example:

Behavior: Employee is continually tardy.

Consequence: You speak with them about their tardiness (negative consequence in your mind).

Antecedent: Employee craves the attention they are getting so they see this as positive reinforcement and continue to be tardy.

Here is another example:

Behavior: Your star employee leads a difficult project really well.

Consequence: They receive your praise and a spot bonus (positive reinforcement in your mind).

Antecedent: If (and this is a big IF) the employee feels positively reinforced by your praise, they will look forward to another project.

However, if they are the person you always turn to because they always deliver results, this praise may be received negatively as they realize it simply means more work for them in the future.

It is critical that the consequence be a positive reinforcement from the recipient's point of view. While it sounds trivial and simple, it isn't. We all do what we do because of what happens to us when we do it. Even when it seems illogical to others, behaviors are always a response to what happened to us. And since we cause change by managing behaviors, this simple A-B-C analysis tool can be very handy for determining "why does someone do what they do".

In healthy organizations, negative behaviors are eliminated by consciously managing consequences. Behaviors are accelerated by providing significantly more positive reinforcement than negative reinforcement (at least a 4:1 ratio and hopefully much higher).

I often encounter adults in positions of leadership and supervision who don't want to try this. They think it is great for their kids, but not for their employees.

They are right - it is great for their kids. We manage our children's behaviors using this A-B-C approach almost subconsciously. And when we provide a lot more positive than negative reinforcement, our kids respond in marvelous ways. So I ask you, if it is good for your family and your children, and it works, why wouldn't you want to use it at work?

While this sounds almost too elementary, managing behaviors through consequences is the root of all behavior modification. As was stated above, culture is the collective set of beliefs and behaviors of our employees so it behooves us as leaders to understand and manage behavior effectively.

My Story

A long time ago I had the privilege of attending a series of workshop with Dr. Aubrey Daniels. He is based in Atlanta and has been the leader in both the research and application of performance management for many years. It is just marvelous to listen to him provide words of wisdom in his easy, Southern, relaxed manner. These are what he calls Pearls of Wisdom and they truly are. He is the first person I remember hearing say "we all do what we do because of what happens to us when we do it". I was puzzled by this statement at first because so many employees (yes, I was an HR manager at the time so I dealt with all sorts of seemingly illogical behaviors) always seemed to be doing things that were illogical from their manager's or my perspective. But Aubrey is right. Behaviors may seem illogical to others, but to the one doing them they make perfect sense.

Thank you, Aubrey, for your gentle way of teaching, your many Pearls of Wisdom, and your vast insight into human behavior. Your wise words have served me well.

Turnaround Success Story

I feel like a proud parent who's 1-year old just took their first steps. I am proud of all of my client's accomplishments and for the privilege of being a part of their growth. There is one in particular, however, I just have to brag about because of the tremendous turn-around of the owner's capability and mindset.

Thinking Caps Design (www.thinkingcaps.net), an environmental graphic design firm that specializes in graphics for the built environment, is achieving results counter to most of the economy today. Owner, Julie Henson, is quick to point out the results and business performance are due to the longevity, creativity, and dedication of the staff who are committed to understanding their client's needs and achieving very effective blends of art and commerce. Thinking Caps has achieved an incredible transformation and in the process the team is bucking much of the negative trend in business today.

When I met Julie several years ago she was in the midst of a transition, doing a lot of soul searching, struggling to work on the business rather than be consumed by it, and wondering about how to best use her strengths. I am delighted to have been able to help Julie create a practical, achievable strategic plan each year and to coach her as a leader and owner, but the real tribute goes to her and the staff at Thinking Caps for their diligence, dedication and just plain hard work.

Here are some of the highlights that demonstrate achievable results when employees know where they are headed, how they can contribute, the results their efforts produce, and when the owner manages effectively with a future focus in mind.

- ✓ The firm is profitable, growing and able to pay year-end bonuses…only 31% of US businesses can afford to pay bonuses and even fewer small businesses do so.

- ✓ The company strategic plan is shared with all the employees so everyone knows what their part is in making the organization successful.

- ✓ All-Staff meetings are held to keep everyone well-informed of company and client needs, and progress. And concerns toward strategic goals are shared.

- ✓ Each staff member receives specific recognition for their unique contributions and how they are contributing to client success, personal growth, and sharing with other staff members.

- ✓ The firm has been recognized with several industry awards all of which were achieved because of team work and collaboration.

- ✓ Financially, loans have been paid off, 401K company matches have been increased, salaries were increased, bonuses are being paid, memberships in professional organizations have been increased, equipment leases have been reduced, computer operating systems have been upgraded, and work flow, proposal development and production monitoring improvement projects are more profitable than in the past.

So amid the gloomy financial headlines, it is possible to turn a profit, have long-term, contributing employees, stay on top of the business rather than buried underneath it, and see bright potential for the future.

My Story

I met Julie as a fellow member of WATT (Women at the Top). We are a group of Phoenix-based business women who meet weekly to network, listen to each other's challenges, provide a sounding board and mirror for one another, and provide supportive encouragement. As always, I feel I am getting more than I am giving. Others tell me it is the other way around, but as long as we all feel like we are getting what we need and providing what others need it is a win/win for all.

Julie is just one example of the intrinsic reward I get from my clients on a daily basis. It is people like Julie and the turnaround stories I have the privilege of being a part of that make being a consultant extremely rewarding. There are days when it would be easier, and frankly a lot more lucrative, to go to work for someone else, but then I would never have met Julie and my life would be less rich.

What are the turnaround stories you see around you? Who in your industry is thriving despite the economic challenges? Are you the example everyone else is admiring?

When is Enough, Enough?

I get so much insight from others and pass it along as wonderful recycled wisdom that sometimes I don't think there is any original thinking in the world. Recently I had this happen with two of my very good friends and business colleagues. One of them said, "We really need to talk about when is enough, enough?" and we decided to have this discussion at our next Master Mind work session. Then on the heels of that proclamation, I received this very insightful message below.

We convince ourselves that life will be better once we are married, have a baby, then another.

Then we get frustrated because our children are not old enough and that all will be well when they are older.

Then we are frustrated because they reach adolescence and we must deal with them. Surely we will be happier when they grow out of the teen years.

We tell ourselves our life will be better when our spouse gets his/her act together, when we have a new car, when we take a vacation, when we finally retire.

The truth is that there is no better time to be happy than right now. If not now, then when?

Your life will always be full of challenges. It is better to admit as much and decide to be happy in spite of it all.

Unknown

Indeed, when is enough, enough? We seem to work all our lives to achieve an illusive something in the future, when maybe the future is now and we simply need to become content. I've always been a very happy, even tempered person, who has enjoyed a great deal of satisfaction with where I was in life at that moment. But even with this general temperament, I do get ahead of myself sometimes and begin focusing on '"if only or when". In reality I simply need to be accepting of the many blessings I have and relish in the contentment of the moment.

One thing that has helped me achieve a greater sense of contentment and balance is to redefine retirement. My redefinition of this state of mind is not a financial position or an age related event it is when you are in a position where you can be doing exactly what you want to be doing. So by this definition we can all be retired whenever and at what age we choose to be.

If we all decided to accept this definition we would all find contentment and satisfaction at any stage in our lives.

My Story

My husband and I have the fabulous habit of trying to play golf together at least once a week. We don't always get this accomplished because client schedules don't always allow us to do so, but we certainly try our best to reserve this time for each other. When we are heading off to the course, I frequently ask him, "Are we practicing retirement?" It is a bit of an inside joke between the two of us because often we don't feel like we can spare the time as there is always work waiting in the office.

But truly, if we don't carve out time for those closest to us and that we care the most about why are we working so hard anyway? And as you know to be good at anything you have to practice so we do need to practice retirement if we are going to be good at it when we get there, right?

So have you practiced retirement lately? Are you carving out enough time for those you care the most about? The work will always be there, but your loved ones may not be. I have to remind myself of important priorities so I manage my activities rather than having the activities manage me. How about you?

Your Employees' Perspective

In the article entitled, *Early Warning Signs*, there is a quiz which helps you assess the organizational health of your company. It included a list of questions which if you answered "No" to any of them indicated a potential organizational health hazard. While I am sure you answered these questions as honestly and accurately as you could from your perspective, the true test is to get answers to these same questions and topics from your employees' perspective. After all, they are your first customer. If you aren't servicing them well, you are not likely to collectively get your ultimate customers serviced very well.

If you are willing to take the risk, consider asking your employees the following questions. Between your own responses in the *Early Warning Signs* quiz and those of your employees from the quiz below, you will have a much fuller picture of your organization's health. The questions have been slightly reworded so they can be answered from your employee's perspective.

<u>Question</u>	<u>Yes/No</u>
<u>Strategy and Governance</u>	
Do you know the Vision, Mission and Guiding Principles or Values for your organization?	_____
Are the Vision, Mission and Guiding Principles or Values statements for your organization publicized?	_____
Does your organization have a strategic plan?	_____
If your organization has a strategic plan is it shared with all employees?	_____
Do you know what your organization's goals are for this year?	_____
If your organization uses metrics to track organizational performance, do you know what the	_____
metrics are?	_____
If the organization has targeted goals and metrics are they shared with all employees?	_____
Are the organization's financial goals integrated with internal processes, customer needs and the development growth of employees?	_____
Do you know if the organization has a governance policy that the Board and senior managers must follow?	_____
<u>Communication</u>	
Do you know what you have to do to help the organization reach it's goals?	_____
Is the progress of your organization toward its goals shared with you throughout the year?	_____
Are communications within your organization meaningful and useful to you?	_____
Are the communication and the messages conveyed consistent through out your organization?	_____
Are there effective methods for employees to communicate up the channel in your organization?	_____
Does information flow freely both up and down the channel?	_____

TIPS: TECHNIQUES, IDEAS, POSSIBILITIES AND SOLUTIONS FOR LEADERS

Leadership Development and Training

Do you receive a performance review at least annually? _____

Do you jointly develop a personal development plan with your supervisor at least annually? _____

Do you receive training each year that is specific to your current job or a position you are preparing for in the future? _____

Does your organization ensure that what is learned gets applied on the job? _____

Does your organization have both supervisory and management training for people in these roles? _____

Do you know if your organization has a succession planning process that identifies key positions and emerging leaders? _____

Do you know if the individuals in the succession plan get specific mentoring, coaching and development in order to be able to step into key roles when needed? _____

Are change efforts led effectively in your organization? _____

From your perspective does the senior leadership team work effectively together? _____

Accountability

In your view, do employees (including managers and supervisors) take responsibility for issues when they come up or are they viewed as "someone else's" problem? _____

Do you know what the job expectations and standards are for your position? _____

Are people at all levels in your organization held accountable for achieving results? _____

Are employees rewarded and recognized for work well done and coached when they need help? _____

Does the organization proactively eliminate those employees who infect others with negative attitudes and who don't contribute? _____

Do those employees who truly are exemplary get the recognition and rewards they deserve? _____

As a manager or business owner it takes courage to ask these questions of your employees and face the answers they give you. What I've found is the number of negative responses is usually higher than anticipated. However, the respect, credibility and trustworthiness for a proactive leader increases significantly for those who are willing to take action to address their employees' concerns. Beware, however, if you ask these questions and then don't take action to address the needs you discover, respect, credibility and trustworthiness will significantly diminish. If you are willing to ask, listen. If you hear, take action.

My Story

It takes courage to ask others for their opinion of ourselves or our leadership performance. But all things in life have some degree of risk and in this case if we are willing to listen to our employees' perspective there will be a healthy dose of reward also. Reward, at least if you are willing to listen and then take action on what you hear.

I have great admiration for one particular client with whom I've been working for eight years. The first piece of work he asked me to provide was an organizational assessment. His words were to the effect of "I believe I know what our challenges are and what our needs are. I think I know what we are good at and where we are failing. But that's just my opinion. I need to know what my employees think because they are the ones who produce the results". Truer words were never spoken, but it takes a leader with courage and broad shoulders to speak them.

So I listened to the employees, I compiled the data, I shared it with the leader and in turn it was shared with all of the employees. That was eight years ago. The leader is still listening, I am still aiding him and the employees and they are still working on their weaknesses. In this case I use weaknesses very loosely. You see they are a world-class organization, but the best always want to get better. They get awards and recognition for their outstanding achievements yet they are constantly striving to push the envelope of excellence further. It all started with the courage to ask the employees their opinion and then together decide how to improve. I am just the lucky one that gets to help them achieve their goals.

CHAPTER 2
Ideas

Building Blocks of Trust

Every business person wants to find that magic elixir that will provide the speed we think we need to gain and even better, a competitive advantage to get where we really think we want to go. I recently read **The Speed of Trust** by Stephen M. R. Covey, PH.D. and while the insights of this book cannot be applied quickly to propel you forward, much of what is presented in the book can yield high dividends over the long term.

You may be familiar with the trust ladder I use to help explain the component parts of trust, how to establish it and how to begin to restore it when trust has been damaged. The essential elements of the trust ladder are below.

Trust Ladder

Risk Taking
Collaboration takes place
Creativity and innovation are more robust
Is a product of the first four steps

Trustworthiness
Has a shelf life
More difficult to build each time it is broken
Is a product of the first three steps

Credibility
Believability through your integrity and intent
Is a product of the first two steps

Agreement
Must be met/kept
Based upon mutual benefit
Is a product of the first step

Understanding
Requires honest, open dialogue
Information is freely shared

Dr. Christian Amoroso, M.D., 1993

I will be forever indebted to Dr. Christian Amoroso for developing this model and sharing it with me in 1993. Now I also am indebted to Dr. Stephen M.R. Covey for adding the **Economics of Trust** to this model.

Have you ever thought you could put a dollar value on the cost of trust? Think again. There is an economic value to the intangible characteristics of trust. In organizations where trust is low, it does take longer to get anything done. Bureaucracy gets in the way, resistance is prevalent, people over promise and under deliver, but in organizations where trust is high, people are willing to innovate, they tolerate mistakes in the spirit of breakthrough learning, people are candid and authentic, and there is palpable energy that comes from accountability and achievement.

Economics of Trust

High	High Trust, Slow Speed = Slow to React Inability to Monetize on Trusting Culture	High Trust, High Speed = High profits, Lower Cost Quickly Capitalize on Trusting Culture
T R U S T L E V E L	Low Trust, Lower Speed = Lower Productivity, Sluggish Performance	Lower Trust, Higher Speed = Lower Profits, Higher Costs
Low	Low	High

Speed of Business

My Story

Toward the latter years of my corporate career, I was a member of the World-Wide Enterprise Resource Planning (ERP) implementation team. My role was to help define, lead and create acceptance for a global computer installation system. While this was the right decision for the company, it caused adverse impact on employees and as the Change Management initiative leader, I had to communicate, convey and build trust. I relied heavily on the materials of Dr. Stephen Covey and the very practical and insightful applications of knowledge of Dr. Christian Amoroso.

Certainly we were all taking an enormous risk as the company was the only company in the world at that time to have undertaken a global installation of computer systems on such a large scale. We felt we had no option since our systems were incompatible with the needs of a global, integrated company. So building trust and confidence were key in not only the acceptance of the change, but the entire viability of the change in the employees' minds.

Creating Win/Win in Tough Situations

In my career as a leadership strategist and organizational consultant, I have often been asked to conduct organizational assessments. I get this request for a variety of reasons, but often it is to discover what the obstacles are within an organization that may be preventing it from achieving its goals or breaking through to the next level of performance. The findings are instructive for the organizational leadership and generally serve as the foundation for future change initiatives.

The toughest situations are those when the primary obstacle is the leader. When this is the case, there is very little win/win in the organization currently. Organizational performance is sub-optimized, employees are usually frustrated, the leader is not as effective as they could be and the messenger runs the risk of being shot. In these cases, everyone says they want improvement, but very frequently the leader is not made aware of the dynamics and impact of his/her actions. So what do you do to make this a win/win situation? Here are some positive steps to consider:

As an employee you can…

- Be the example of what you want others to be - step up to personal leadership.

- Provide honest input when asked through an employee survey or a 360 degree assessment process.

- Realize you can only control you own behaviors – you do not own the actions of others.

As a management peer/friend you can…

- Help the leader see how much the organization cares about and depends on their continued ability to be a strong leader.

- Encourage the use of a 360 degree assessment process, if it is not currently used, so the leader gets honest input from multiple perspectives.

- Ask the leader to mentor you so that as a protégé you have the opportunity to show them a mirror image of what you wish they were and are in a position to discuss a wide variety of situations with them privately.

As a consultant you can …

- Help the leadership team see the value of using 360 degree assessment processes including providing coaching for the participants.

- Have the courage to be honest with the leader in a tactful, kind, caring manner.

- Use a variety of instruments and/or processes to help not only the leader, but also the leadership team deal with the challenges of effective leadership.

- Develop a coaching rather than a consulting relationship with the leader and/or the whole leadership team .

As the leader being confronted you can…

- Recognize you have both a personal responsibility and an enterprise responsibility to be an effective leader.

- Realize your management peer/friends, many of your employees and your consultant are allies in your effort.

- Initiate a leadership development and growth process for the entire leadership team.

- Demonstrate the courage it takes to confront change both personally and as the primary change leader for the enterprise.

My Story

More often than not, I found myself needing to convey a message to the organizational leader, who often was also my primary client, that was not a message they wanted to hear. They had asked me to conduct an organizational assessment to figure out how to "fix" their organization and what they were going to find out is the "fix" needed to start with themselves. This isn't a surprise because in large part organizations are simply a complex reflection of their leadership.

In one very difficult situation two other colleagues and I were providing feedback to three individuals who jointly owned a large printing company in the south western US. Two of the owners were very attuned to the needs of the organization and the impact they were having on the organization. The third owner was either oblivious or in denial. As we continued to review the findings of our assessment, this owner gradually turned his back to us until he was completed turned around and looking out the window. Clearly he was hearing the words we were speaking, but was in denial about the message. We completed the feedback session as two of the owners were fully engaged and wanted to hear the findings.

To make a long story shorter, the third owner called us back two weeks later and admitted he couldn't hear the message because his emotions were blocking his acceptance. However, he realized he needed to change himself, and if the organization was to change, he needed to step up to leading the change effort. He asked if we would come back and review the findings again as he now was in a position to hear what we had to say. While this example is extreme the inability to truly hear what needs to be heard is common when we don't want to hear the message.

Economic Value of Trust

Economic value and trust may seem like strange bedfellows at first glance. But when you look deeper, you see that for people and organizations where trust is prevalent decisions are made more quickly, operations run more smoothly and with greater ease, and therefore, with less cost than those where trust is low or where distrust is prevalent. It is easy to both feel and see the impact trust, or the lack of it, has on organizational and personal effectiveness. Consider these two contrasting lists as examples. (See also the Building Blocks of Trust article earlier in this book.)

Low Trust Behaviors

* People manipulate and distort facts.

* People withhold information or hoard it.

* Getting and taking credit is very important.

* Spin is added to get advantage.

* There are meetings before and after meetings.

* Excuses accompany expectations.

High Trust Behaviors

* Information is open, honest and freely shared.

* Mistakes are tolerated as a way of learning.

* People share credit for successes.

* Talk is straight; real issues are confronted.

* Transparency and authenticity are practiced and valued.

* There is a high degree of accountability.

Now couple these behavioral dynamics with economic value and you can quickly see the financial advantage high-trust organizations have over those where distrust exists. Consider these formulas:

$$\downarrow \textbf{Trust} = \downarrow \textbf{Speed} \uparrow \textbf{Cost} \qquad \text{while} \qquad \uparrow \textbf{Trust} = \uparrow \textbf{Speed} \downarrow \textbf{Cost}$$

If you have worked with me to develop your strategic plan you can relate to the formula of S x E = R (Strategy times Execution equals Results). But consider this even more powerful formula:

(S x E) T = R which is ({Strategy times Execution} multiplied by Trust equals Results)

Success in business requires both a great strategy and great execution, but distrust can destroy both. High trust won't rescue a poor strategy, but low trust will almost always undermine a good one. So you can see the multiplicative impact trust has on your potential to achieve results – this is the Economic Value of Trust!

Here are two opposing cases which point out the real dollars and cents of the economic value of trust.

The Sarbanes-Oxley Act was passed in response to situations like Enron, WorldCom, and other corporate scandals which demonstrated poor ethics and spawned distrust. Conservative estimates for the cost of implementation to date are estimated to be $35 billion. Contrast this with Warren Buffet who has such trust in his business dealings that he recently made a major acquisition from McLane Distribution for $23 billion on the basis of one two-hour meeting, zero due diligence, and a hand shake. Maybe you aren't involved in billion-dollar deals, but you nonetheless are bearing the cost of distrust or reaping the rewards of your trusting environment.

While I'd like to have been wise enough to have developed the formulas I've shared with you, alas I am only wise enough to read the work of and associate with others more wise than I. The credit goes to Dr. Stephen M. R. Covey for his recent book, *The Speed of Trust,* upon which I founded this article.

My Story

One of my life's beliefs is that you have to give away trust before you get it back. I have seen this demonstrated hundreds of times in my work as an internal and external consultant. The heart of being an Organizational Development consultant is being able to have an honest, heart-to-heart dialog with people at any level of the organization about either their personal needs and opportunities or the needs and opportunities for the organization. Only rarely was I unable to very quickly get the person to open up and be very forthright with me about what was going on, what they felt was needed, and how I might be able to assist. As a consultant, I can't help if I can't get this conversation to occur.

Looking back on those rare occasions when I just couldn't seem to establish rapport with a person, it was because I, for one reason or another, didn't give trust to the other individual. You can't see trust, but you certainly can feel it. And the feeling is strong when trust is absent. Transparency and authenticity are the bedrock of giving trust to others and being a trustworthy person yourself.

Five P's of Organizational Leadership

Mental models help us remember critical concepts. One mental model I use daily consists of the **Five P's of Organizational Leadership**. The Five P's are the backbone of all organizational structures. By analyzing each of these individually and also as an interdependent system, the root causes of many organizational challenges and performance concerns can be determined. Change any of the five and you inherently change the whole so both independent and interdependent analysis is required.

Every organizational analysis I have ever done has been based upon this simple, yet complete model. The more organizational leaders understand the interdependence of these five dynamics the more they will increase their leadership capability. Leading without understanding these five key functions and the interdependence of them, often leads to increased ineffectiveness.

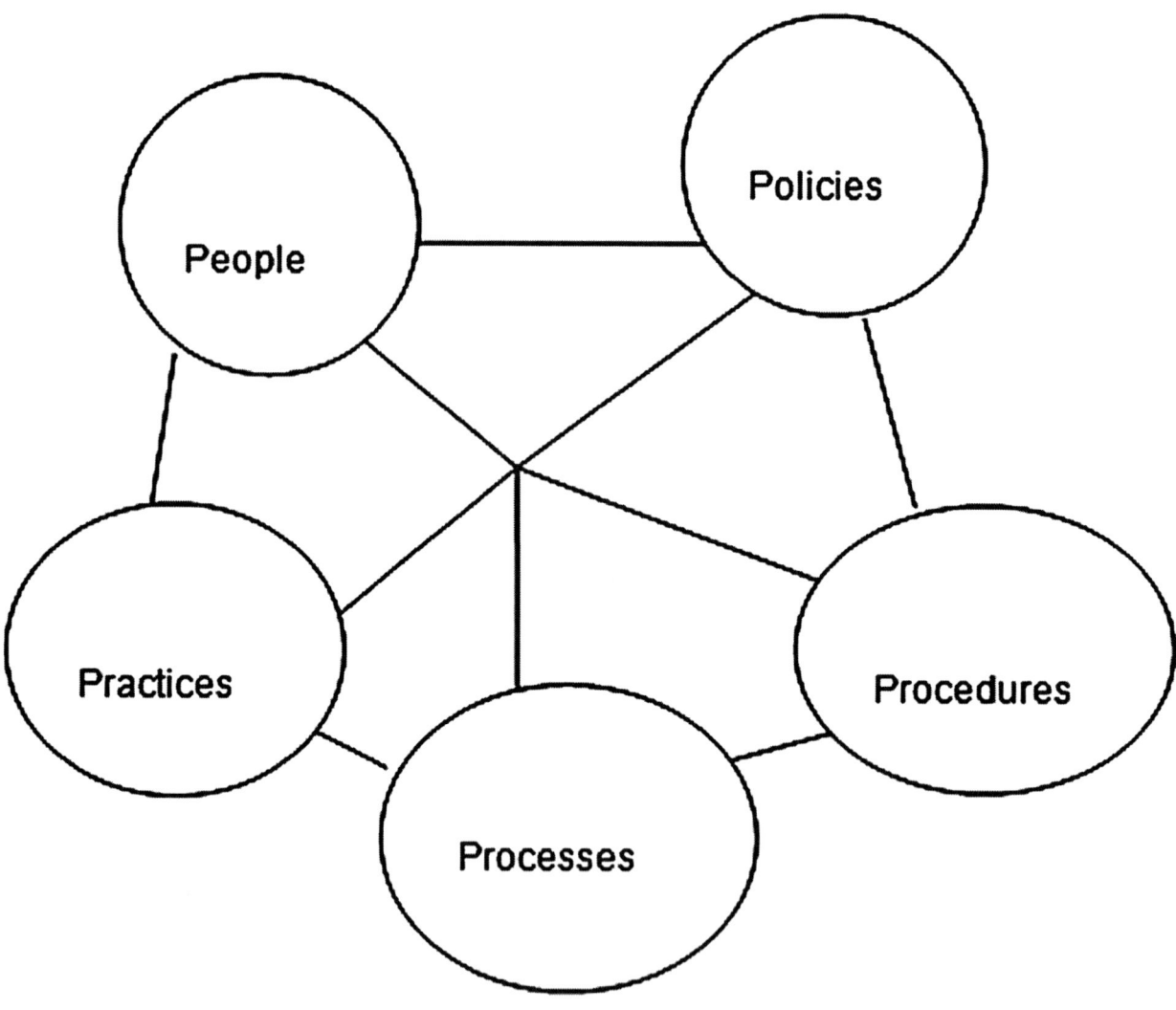

Five P's of Organizational Leadership

People

As the phrase goes, get the right people on the bus and get the wrong people off. No matter what profession or industry you are in, all of your products and services are delivered through your staff. So Rule Number 1 is "get the right people on the bus" and make sure they know where the company is going and how they can help the organization succeed.

Policies

Policies are those formalized, written "rules to live by" within a company. They specify **WHAT**. Keep them simple, easy to understand, logical and as few as necessary to be effective. In general, the more you get the right people on the bus, the fewer policies you need.

Practices

Practices are the collective habits and actions that tell people **WHAT** and **HOW** to do and not do, but they are not written. They are what people see and hear, not what they read.

Procedures

Procedures are written sets of instructions that tell people **HOW** to do specific tasks. They are often used as training aids and help achieve consistency.

Processes

Systems, structures, infrastructures all have processes that define both **HOW** and **WHAT**.

(See also article entitled Take Care of the Culture, Everything Else Will Follow in this book).

My Story

The KISS (Keep It Short and Simple!) principle works well so why should we make things overly complicated? I've often said my profession isn't difficult, but it certainly is a lot of hard work. So in the spirit of trying to keep things simple, very early on in my career I developed the 5 P's as a mental guide for quickly analyzing situations in organizations.

If you aren't getting the results you want then one or more of the 5 P's is either missing or misaligned. And if you are getting the results you want, I'm pretty certain the 5 P's are well balanced. So while you probably won't find these same 5 P's in any OD or management text book, they served me well for 40 years as a quick mental model for analyzing the functionality of organizations.

Give It Away – a Growth Strategy

Yep, that's right! You gotta' give it away to get it back. Sounds kind of like reverse logic and it is in some ways, but many things in life compound themselves many fold only after you give them away.

Love   Trust   Friendship   Wisdom   Service

These and many more things must be given away before you get them back!

Ever notice how when you smile at someone they generally smile back. When you speak first, the recipient responds. When you do a kindly deed, one will come back to you. I have a good friend, Silver Rose, who speaks on the Law of Attraction, based upon this principle. You get what you focus on. So when you give love, trust others, bestow friendship, share wisdom, provide service it comes right back to you like a boomerang.

I use this same strategy to grow my business. I'll bet it would work for you too, but you have to be willing to "give before you get". Let me give you an example. I gave away $10,000 dollars in service to a client in order to get back $2,500 a month. I had a break even point in four months. Would you make that kind of investment?

A few years ago, I decided the best way I could grow my business was by meeting members of Boards of Directors. My logic was that they were the kind of people who owned businesses, could afford to hire me, and understood the value of and how to effectively use consultants. So I volunteered to design and facilitate the Board retreats for a major employer in our area. I knew I'd have to give away service, but I hoped in return I would meet potential clients and be able to influence their decision to use my services. After several conversations with the President of the organization, it was clear there was long-term interest in using my services not for the Board, but for the organization it governed. I am still working with this client and they provide me wonderful referrals to other potential clients.

I just did it again. I just offered pro bono services to one of the clients they referred me to. Yet again, I believe if I give it away, I'll get it back. I can't be a philanthropist of money, but I can be a philanthropist of talent and service and, sure enough, I get paid back in friendship, a larger, richer community and business network, and business growth.

What I focus on is identifying who are good prospects. Who are the business leaders who believe in returning value for value given? Who believe in the law of attraction and have something I need in return.

Try it! I guarantee the more you give away wisdom, friendship, love, trust and service the more you will get it back.

My Story

I think I got this belief from my Dad. He gave away love, smiles, friendship and great business advise his whole life. The best role models simply live their beliefs and they rub off on others. This is what happened to me. My Dad wasn't one for verbalizing his feelings very openly, but he demonstrated his friendship, love and caring in everything he did. So it was easy for me to learn that if you gave it away, you get it back. What unwritten messages are you giving away to others?

If You're Happy and You Know It - Clap Your Hands

"If you're happy and you know it, clap your hands

If you're happy and you know it, clap your hands

If you're happy and you know it, then your life will surely show it,

If you're happy and you know it, clap your hands!"

Remember this little camp song? I spend the summer months living two miles from my young granddaughter so I hear these kinds of songs frequently. These songs along with a conversation over coffee at the end of our neighborhood bike ride recently caused me to reflect on the fundamental differences our lives can take when we make well thought-out, future-focused decisions versus leading an unplanned, laissez faire type of life.

Certainly our lives in general as well as our attitudes and outlooks demonstrate to others our happiness and contentment or the lack thereof. And, in turn, serve to continually reinforce and reinvigorate our life views and, consequently, become self-fulfilling prophecies. The degree of satisfaction with life in general and our careers specifically are a direct result of the choices we make. But how can we ensure the choices we make are the right ones and that they will collectively result in producing a full, satisfying, rewarding professional and personal life?

I contend that making values-based decisions is one of the keys to finding happiness. Here are some of life's lessons resulting from making value-based decisions from our bike group's conversation.

Lesson one – Perspective

One fellow cyclist is a trial attorney whose day job is filled with high pressure, top-tier clients whom he defends. He keeps the deadlines and pressure of his partners and clients in perspective by focusing on the future day job he is building toward. While his partners' lives are entirely consumed by and defined by their careers, they have little family life, poor relationships with their children and few outside interests. While my friend likes his chosen profession, it is a means to an end which for him is enjoying the full and rewarding life he has with his spouse, children, and friends. His well balanced life along with the good planning he is doing now will allow him to be the mountain biking paramedic he wants to be. Let's hope none you need his skills on your mountain bike rides, but just in case, he'll be there to patch up your skinned knees and bumped elbows and hopefully no injuries worse than these.

Lesson two – Values over Dollars

Another of my fellow cyclists is a VP of HR for a very large national insurance company. He was recently offered a corporate position at headquarters which, of course, meant an increase in salary and promotion, but also meant moving, disrupting his family, and (this is the kicker) moving operations off-shore. He turned it down. While moving the operations off shore was the right decision from a corporate financial perspective, he could foresee the adverse impact on US employees and, in particular, a decreased level of customer service. Skip ahead a few months…he is now experiencing the results of that decision. His phone and email are full of complaints and he has to deal daily with the drama of the situation.

After a year of living with complaints and watching service deteriorate, he is now in the midst of very positive interviews for a new position with a different company. He will need to move his family, but will gain peace of mind, professional integrity, fewer complaints and a happy family. He knows his decision to change companies is the right one for him, his family and their relationships. His value-based decision allows him to sleep peacefully at night.

Lesson three – Creating new Traditions

Sometimes life provides opportunities shrouded in non-traditional trappings. This is the case of another one of my cycling friends. In this case the financial and the value-based reasons for the decision were congruent. Mom is a radiologist, Dad has an MBA. Both were very successfully employed, but when it came time to start a family, they decided Mom had more earning power and Dad was well-suited for raising the kids. This is a match made in heaven as both spouses are flourishing and so are the kids. What a treat to have a Dad go on the school trip with you rather than just the Moms getting involved. I'm sure there are days when it isn't easy for Mom to be the breadwinner and I'm positive there are days that Dad would rather go to the office than do the laundry and grocery shopping, but in the end the decision to lead through a non-traditional role has made this family a winner all around.

So, if you're happy and you know it, clap your hands!

My Story

Life is too short to live it unhappily. I grew up in a home that was full of love and caring yet in many ways was extremely dysfunctional. (But what is normal anyway?) I learned early on that amid conditions that you can't control yourself, you often have to figure out how to make your own happiness. We sometimes can't control the cards that life deals to us, but we can control how we play our cards. As a result, I always seem to find the brighter side of things and in the process, hopefully, I help others see the brighter side of things themselves.

Lessons from the Non-Profit World – The Virtues of Stewardship

Stewardship is a word we don't seem to use in the for-profit business world. I don't believe I've ever heard that word used or the concept even talked about among any of my for-profit clients. Yet, almost every time I work with one of my not-for-profit clients I hear the word and the concept throughout our conversations particularly, when I am working with my philanthropic clients. So if the concept of stewardship is so important to the non-profit world wouldn't you think there is something the for-profit world could learn from them? You bet there is.

So what is stewardship anyway? In simple terms in the philanthropic world, it is all the attention given to donor's in-between donations and the beneficent utilization of the funds given to them by those donors. They get money from donors who are, in fact, their customers. Isn't that what you do in your for-profit world also...get money from customers in exchange for a service or product? One of the cornerstones of the most successful philanthropic organizations is the effective stewarding of funds and stewardship toward their donors. They don't get repeat business without it. In their world, stewardship looks like...

- Making phone calls and sending thank you letters to donors within 24 hours of receipt.

- Differentiated recognition based upon the amount, consecutive years given and specific interests of the donor.

- Special events to recognize faithfulness and continued support.

- Special services extended to those who are most generous.

- Reporting back to donors (customers) about how their funds were used.

- Special reports and publications sent to donors in recognition of their support while explaining how the funds were used to benefit the receiving organization.

- Tours of facilities are provided.

- Personalized holiday and birthday cards are sent, etc.

- And there are hundreds more examples.

I contend that stewardship is also the root of repeat business in the for-profit world, but we don't talk about it in those terms or think about stewardship toward our clients or customers. I contend that we should do so.

In the for-profit world we call these functions customer service. However, this phrase is very overused and in some cases has bad connotations. I think we would be wise to begin thinking in terms of stewardship toward our clients and customers and stewarding their loyalty to us. Stewardship is a great word to include in our business conversations.

Each year one of the key initiatives in my strategic plan is to very intentionally be a steward for my loyal clients by providing each of them very personalized service, reporting to them on the value they provide to my business, listening to them and telling them what I've specifically done with their suggestions. I am also very conscious of the obligation I have to each of them as unique contributors to my success. What do your stewardship activities need to be for your clients? How are you showing appreciation to them for their repeat business? Is stewardship a concept you are actively integrating into your business methods?

My Story

I'll admit I am like most of the people I wrote about in this article in that I never thought about stewardship being an important part of business behavior. Having worked for two extremely large global corporations in my life, of course, I had customer service drilled into my corporate psyche. But there is a subtle, yet critical difference between customer service and stewardship.

I realized this only after I started working with a large healthcare firm that believes in and lives stewardship for their donors in a world-class manner. Stewardship is not just about knowing clients and serving them well; it is about giving back and diligently stewarding the gifts we receive from them. I know in the for-profit world we don't see the payments received for services or products as gifts, but in fact they are. As I began to see payment for my services as gifts from my clients, I began to serve them differently, better, and in a more reciprocal manner. I became a steward of our relationship rather than just a provider of services.

Life is a White Board

Every once in a while we experience something in our lives that puts things into focus. Something that helps us re-balance our priorities and reassess our world. Calamities like a flood, a fire, an accident, a death, a near miss or some other unexpected catastrophe.

My family experienced this a few summers ago when the Four Mile Canyon fire was raging just west of our home in Colorado. The water-bearing helicopters and retardant slurry bombers didn't stop for days and the air was filled with acrid smoke and ash. We stayed focused on the positive in that we had no direct damage and while there were millions of dollars in property damage, there were no injuries from this fire. I heard one of the victims who lost his home say in a newspaper interview that "Life is a White Board" and his had just been erased clean.

It seems to me this is an apt metaphor for those times in our lives when we are caused to stop and reevaluate. Rather than focusing on the life that was there a second ago that just got erased, maybe we should focus on ensuring the white board always has written on it what is most enduring, most endearing and most valuable to us.

As this gentleman went on to say, it wasn't the stuff he would miss, it was the memories. His family was fine and he could rebuild, but he would always long for the ancient Mayan ruin items he found in South America and he would always long for treasures he brought back from Egypt. Now he will concentrate on the treasures he has with him that are dear and enduring which are his family, his health and his life.

I'm wondering what is written on your White Board of Life. Is it something worth preserving through your actions and deeds or is it something more fleeting and less substantial. I know I sometime get caught up in the day-to-day scribbles on my own White Board and lose sight of the messages I most want my family, friends and colleagues to know and always remember about me.

Now is a good time to assess as the clouds are moving in and we have a 40% change of rain to help the fire fighters get forest fires throughout the west under control.

My Story

Maybe it is just age or maybe it is wisdom or maybe it is just coincidence, but the metaphor of life being a white board is poignant for me. White boards are prevalent in offices these days for capturing group ideas, diagramming options, reworking what didn't work, etc. They are easily wiped clean and are fresh and ready to re-use. Certainly we can't erase the memories of circumstances quite as quickly as we can erase a White Board, but the metaphor of "getting over it, moving on, not getting stuck, finding a better way or a different solution" works well for me especially when I need to put on my change management hat for my own life and for counseling my clients.

Musings on Working At Home

I have a good friend and business colleague who authored the original version of these musings and they were just too good not to share with you. She encourages those of us who receive her newsletter to pass along and share so I want to be very clear that this article originated and is mostly authored by Billi Lee, The Savvy Institute. Look her up on www.thesavvyinstitute.com. Thanks Billi!

I think the topic of "working from home" is poignant because I have many friends who, due to our age and/or circumstances, are leaving corporate America at around the mid-century mark and are searching for what they will do with their time and professional expertise. For others, it is a choice to establish their careers with a profession that can be managed by working from home. In each case, people are looking for productive contribution and flexibility.

Home offices are the rage. Every model home has one. They are tasteful, well-decorated, and have art objects on every available surface. But they are not functional.

Some of my work-from-home buddies keep strict schedules, some work only when the mood strikes. Some dress professionally while some are sights to behold. Some totally separate their personal and family from their professional side while others negotiate big deals while cooking the family meal amid family chaos. The style matters not. To work at home successfully you have to be a work-at-home kind of person.

Here are Billi's (and my) "Rules for Working from Home"...

- ✓ You have to like, no...relish, your own company. Hours alone can be lonely. You can be very socially skilled, but you have to work best in solitude.

- ✓ You have to love your work. No one has to motivate you or reward you or compliment you. You do what you do because you love it. Working is something you choose to do, it is internally imposed.

- ✓ You have to be your own boss. You have to have the vision, set the direction, provide the feedback, do the strategic thinking, and be responsible for the business. You are "You, Inc."

- ✓ You have to be your own supervisor. You have to do what it takes to get the job done, schedule the time, show up, and produce. It takes discipline, even if the discipline appears to be disorderly.

Like other trends, the home office will eventually give way to the next model home trend, just like the Nordic Track in most homes serves as a second closet. The truth is many people shouldn't work at home, they simply need what the office or factory provides – structure and social interaction as well as the reward of work well done.

So don't fall in love with a stylish home office unless you are already in love with what you do and already find the time and the space to do it, on your own, at home. Otherwise, you'd better leave that spare bedroom alone.

My Story

If you are familiar with the Myers-Briggs Type Indicator assessment you'll know what I mean when I say I am an ISTJ (Introverted, Sensing, Thinking, Judging). In a nutshell, this means that I get my source of energy internally rather than externally, I learn and take in information via my senses more than through my intuition, I make decisions based upon criteria and analysis more than based on my feelings, and I organize the things around me and my life in a more precise and judicious manner rather than in a free-flowing manner.

Those of you who know me well probably are scratching your head about that first characteristic…introversion.   You are right in that to you I appear to be more extroverted because when we are interacting it is in an extroverted, interactive manner. But truth be known, I am a 50/50 mix of introversion and extroversion. To be both happy and productive I need a balance of quiet, introverted time and interactive, social extroverted time.

Now that was a rather long introduction, but it is an important factor when you consider working from home. I need that 50/50 mix of introversion and extroversion so I can't spend all day in the office alone. I need to have alone time to design, analyze, prepare, write, research, etc., but I have to balance that need with being with clients, socializing, etc. If I have too much alone time, I'll simply go to Starbucks for a coffee in order refuel my energy levels.

So consider your personal type before deciding if working from home is right for you. If you need a balance, find a way to get professional camaraderie, social interaction, and client engagement.

Networking as a Successful Tool

I've always been a believer in networking. As a small business owner, my reputation and trusting relationships are at the core of my business growth and my success. In addition to referral business, my network is my primary source of marketing. Recently, I've become more acutely aware of how valuable my personal network is to my happiness and my success. I've also become aware that I have to join the cyber generation in order to use more technically savvy methods of networking.

Master Mind

For 7 years now, a group of other female, small business owners and I have served as a Board of Advisors for one another through a Master Mind group. Each year we develop our business strategies during a 2-day retreat and we meet monthly to review our progress and seek counsel from one another. We have not only become trusted business advisors for one another, we have also become friends, travel companions, and confidantes.

If you are a business owner particularly, if you are a small business owner, you need a similar group. Examine your own situation. Who can you share your fears, hopes, problems, and triumphs with in complete confidence and trust? Who will have the courage to point out when you might be over looking something important or when you have blinders on that may prevent you from seeing the opportunities or barriers in front of you? If you find you need to create a Master Mind group, keep these guidelines in mind as you select your trusted advisors:

- Select only those you trust without question and with whom you hold common values.

- Select people who are willing to share their viewpoint especially when it is different than your own.

- Include members from a variety of professions – they will help you get out of your box and they will also help you expand your sphere of influence as you share contacts with each other.

- Include only those who have impeccable reputations in their own right as their reputations will have an impact on your own.

- From a practical perspective, keep the group small (4-5 people) because face-face meetings are critical to the success of Master Mind. So the larger the group the harder it is to schedule meetings.

As a part of the **Strategic Planning for Entrepreneur's** workshops I facilitate, I work hard to create a Master Mind group for the participants by including 6 follow-up sessions with the participants through which they build not only accountability to use the plans they have developed in the workshop, but they also build a bond and depth of trust. Often they choose to become a Master Mind group in order to carry on support for one another. Many of the Master Mind groups that have been started as a result of these workshops are still supporting one another several years after formation.

Where do you find support for your business? Who provides valuable counsel for you? Who do you trust to hold the mirror for you as a reflection of where you are going and how you are getting there? If you believe a Master Mind group would be beneficial for you, who do you know that meets the qualifications above?

My Story

Years ago my husband was in a Master Mind group with a group of fellow Rotary members. At the time we were owners of a retail triathlon shop in town. He found great benefit in sharing challenges and successes with other business owners as they learned together to run their businesses successfully, overcome common problems, and stretch themselves as they grew year after year.

One of the first people I met when we moved from Colorado to Arizona was Deb Waitkus, founder of Golf for Cause. She invited me to join a new Master Mind group and I knew from my husband's experience that I would benefit greatly. As the article mentions above, we are about to start year 8 of growing, learning, smiling, laughing and sometimes crying together, but through it all we know we are better business owners because of our sharing and support for one another.

Options as we Age

Despite the general doom and gloom we often hear in the news, we do have some positive options in front of us. The challenge is figuring out the best choices among all the options. Life is all about choices and just because we age and supposedly get wiser, the choices don't seem to get any easier. I'm talking about how to most optimally use our productive years as we look beyond the traditional 40-hour work week.

This choice for you may be years away, but it is getting closer. The closer these options get the more we realize the importance of this decision. Of course, you can always continue to use your time as an employee or business owner. The option to continue doing what you are doing is always available. Much has been written recently about the adverse impact on workplaces and our economy by the looming retirement of many baby boomers, so the choice to continue working is welcomed by many employees and employers. However, even if you elect to continue your current employment, consider taking on a mentor role, or document the processes that are the foundation of your organization's success, or become a champion of your organization's knowledge sustainability. One of the primary deficits of boomers retiring is the loss of institutional knowledge, so figure out a way to create a repository or living legacy of organizational knowledge.

As we age we realize that not only do the choices become more important, the opportunity to try new things becomes more precious. What are other alternatives that might allow you to continue to grow and give back to your community and the generations that follow? Different financial demands and having an empty nest provide both greater economic and time flexibility.

As you ponder your options consider…

- Rather than focusing almost exclusively on being an economic capitalist, this is an opportunity to become a philanthropic capitalist by volunteering, and by reinvesting your time, knowledge and energy. Where might you volunteer your time and knowledge that matches both your interests and your community needs?

- Is this the time to explore that hobby or different career you've kept at bay all these years? Now might be the opportune time to learn something new and still remain employed, but in a totally different capacity or area of interest.

- A lot of research shows the more we keep our minds active and growing the more we generally avoid memory loss. How about learning a new language or totally new skill? Do you want to get a degree or explore a whole new subject area?

- You may be in the situation where you have more time than money so being a philanthropist of your time may be ideal for you. Give of your talent and skill, but do so working at no-cost or a lower rate for a not-for profit organization. While you are giving of your time, you function more as a full or part-time employee rather than as a volunteer who occasionally assists the organization.

- Give back by serving in the executive service core in your area. Often either the Chamber of Commerce or the Small Business Administration sponsor groups of seasoned individuals who serve as advisors and consultants to their members.

No matter how you decide to use your time as you age, choose well! You are what you choose to be!

My Story

In this case my story is simple…I am aging. So just like everyone else who reaches a certain point in time, I am reflecting on what's next. I've found as I reflect over my life that about every 3 years I did something new. Sure I was at the same employer for 27 years, but in that span of time I had seven different positions with different sets of responsibilities. I continue to reinvent myself every few years so it is natural for me to wonder what is next. It's just how I grow and live my life. I'm thinking of learning Italian. How about you? What is next for you?

Philanthropist Regardless of Your Wealth

Part of the proverbial American dream is to be wealthy enough to be considered a philanthropist. Oh, to be Carnegie, a Rockefeller, a Buffett or a Gates. Alas, statistically it isn't likely that many of us will achieve this lofty level of wealth, but that doesn't mean we can't be philanthropists of another type. I contend there are many ways to be philanthropic regardless of our wealth. I have long considered myself a philanthropist of time more than of money.

While there have been many times in my life that I would truly have enjoyed being a member of the mega-wealthy crowd, actually becoming a member isn't very likely. I have often wished I had enough wealth to be able to spontaneously buy just the right thing when I spot it for friends, family and acquaintances. One of life's real pleasures for me is spotting the right thing, purchasing it and seeing the sparkle and joy in the recipient's eye's when you know it is just the right gift received as a surprise. So I have often wished for wealth so I could provide surprise treats for friends. Gifting in this manner gives me pleasure by seeing the pleasure it provides others.

I know both intellectually and emotionally when I give of my time in service to others, my giving is compounded many times. Just like in monetary compound interest, the donation of my time is compounded many times through the additional services it provides to others in need. In this way I see myself as a philanthropist of time rather than money. And no matter what our monetary wealth, if we each give of our time, we compound the initial benefit.

I also see myself as a social venture capitalist. Typically, venture capitalists provide financial assistance to aspiring, worthy causes in order to develop, market, produce or sell their ideas, services or products. I am a non-financial venture capitalist. I give my time to worthy causes who in turn fulfill needs in society that I can't directly fulfill myself. Again, I can be a philanthropist without being wealthy by finding ways to compound the benefit of my offering and thus multiply the value others receive.

What are you passionate about? What unmet needs do you see around you that you have the skill and knowledge to aid? What unmet needs can you fulfill and not spend money doing it? What would you fund if you had the mega-wealth of financial philanthropists? If you were wealthy, what organizations would you donate to? What needs do these organizations have that you have the talent to help fulfill? I know there are needs all around us that we often don't see because we haven't trained ourselves to look for the opportunities and/or we haven't chosen to see ourselves as philanthropists or social venture capitalists in a non-financial way.

Warren Buffett and the Gates are challenging the Forbes 400 wealthiest people in the world to give huge portions of their wealth during their life times. This is not only a US challenge, but a world challenge. Imagine the difference in our social issues, society in general, the financial spin-off effect and the sense of well-being throughout the world if this happens. But also imagine the same social impact if each of us began to see ourselves as social venture capitalists and philanthropists of our time and talent regardless of our wealth. What a difference each offering can make when it is compounded millions of times.

I challenge you to find one unmet need around you, offer your assistance, and find true pleasure in offering your skill, talent or service. If each reader of this article did this there would already be a huge social impact. I hope Buffett and the Gates are successful in their challenge to their wealthy friends, and I also hope I am successful in challenging each of you to find and fulfil an unmet need that feeds your passion.

Just imagine the possibilities our collective gifts will make. It's good for society, it makes the world a better place, it's good for business, and you'll be feeding your soul.

My Story

Success breeds success! This is an adage I'm sure you've heard before and I believe it. If you want to be successful, be around successful people. If you want to learn new things, hang around people who are educating themselves. So if I want to be a philanthropist…be able to help others, give away what I have for the benefit of others…I have to associate with philanthropists and give away what I have. So I joined Social Venture Partners and I continue to work with a not-for-profit Foundation. I learn how others amassed their wealth, what their passions are, what causes they care about and along the way I become richer in spirit and friendships.

Reasons to Hire Big Company Employees

OK, I'm being defensive in this article and I admit it. When I read an article in Entrepreneur Magazine entitled *Should You Hire Workers From Big Companies?* authored by Chris Penttila I just couldn't help my reaction. Not only do I disagree with the author's arguments made for not hiring workers from larger companies, I believe there are very compelling reason to seek out these workers. A large number of the workers available to hire have large-company experience and because of this experience they bring very valuable assets to their next employer.

Ms. Pentilla in her article sites the following reasons as 'red flags' when hiring from Corporate America.

➢ Their cover letter isn't personalized to your firm.

➢ They are more interested in the 401(k) and severance package than having an equity stake translated as they lack ownership and commitment.

➢ They expect travel perks, expense accounts and personal assistants.

➢ They aren't computer savvy.

➢ They expect to be assigned rather than take initiative.

➢ They view meetings as the way to get things done.

➢ They lack the interpersonal skills necessary in a small office.

I simply don't find this to be the case. In fact, based upon conversations I've had with fellow colleagues who spent years in Corporate America we believe workers from big companies offer far more advantages to employers than disadvantages.

Consider these "green flag" reasons to hire those with larger corporate experience.

➢ Almost no one relies on a company 401(k) heavily any more. Workers from all sizes of companies, especially larger firms, realize their best insurance is helping their current employer be successful. Employees from the larger firms more than any other category have been disillusioned by the unfulfilled promises of 401(k) in the past.

➢ Doing more with less has been the mantra of large corporations for the past two decades – these employees will expect nothing less than more of the same at smaller firms.

➢ From the shop floor to the top floor workers from every level of the corporation are well equipped with computer skills. It is almost impossible to run a large firm today without everyone having computer literacy. Larger firms often provide at least 30-40 hours of training per year including computer skills training. Find out what these candidates have been learning and take advantage of their knowledge and education in your firm.

➢ Workers from large firms know the only way you really get work done is through teamwork and collaboration with others. While some individuals may lack interpersonal skills this is true in all organizations just as there are those with highly developed interpersonal skills in any size organization.

➢ Employees from large firms have often been in leadership roles and aren't afraid to step up to responsibility and be accountable for results – producing results and meeting bottom line goals are the primary way you meet performance expectations in corporations. Owners and Wall Street demand it. Embrace the leadership and accountability these employees bring to your firm.

➢ While all employees prefer clarity and specific direction, employees from larger firms are accustomed to achieving results amid ambiguity – knowing how to achieve results amid today's uncertainly is a real asset.

If you are in the fortunate position of being able to hire and the qualifications of candidates are equal, consider the many benefits you'll receive by hiring employees from larger firms. However, in every situation and regardless of the size firm the candidates have worked for in the past, hire the person best suited for your position. You are better off having an empty position than to hire the wrong person.

Just reflect on the anguish and frustration both you and the employees have experienced when you have had to weave your way through managing a troublesome employee who was a good person, but in the wrong job. Make sure you have good processes for getting the right people into the right position, but don't discount the vast skill set those from larger corporations have to offer.

My Story

I've often told my husband I should be paying my former employer rather than receiving a pension from them. Don't get me wrong. I really like getting payment for the years I spent there, but I know I am a better person and a far better consultant for the years of work and knowledge I got from being their employee. The learning, education, experiences and growth I received are priceless to me. So I have no hesitation in recommending hiring others who bring these same types of benefits to their future employers.

Successful Organizational Leadership Requires Conceptualization and Systemic Thinking

The higher you go in an organization the more the skill set needed changes from technical competence to the broader skill of conceptualization. Getting in the door requires technical knowledge of your chosen field, the right attitude and the inherent characteristics valued by the hiring organization. The first several positions you hold are quite likely to be based upon your knowledge, job skill and the ability to delivery specific results. Results get you promoted to higher and higher levels, but at some point the skill set requirements change.

Leading an organization requires the ability to conceptualize about the issues and concerns of an organization, as well as, what is needed in the future. Conceptualization is about being able to see that which is not there. The ability to look at a set of actual circumstances and see beyond them in order to determine the problem or opportunity they present. This skill is about recognizing how the functions of an organization are interdependent; how changes in one area impact all the others.

Conceptualization is critical both in solving today's problems, as well as, anticipating the needs of the market and then having the solution prepared in time to capture the opportunity. For example, the ability to see customers' needs and project the solution in not-yet-developed products or services your organization can provide. In short, the more senior the role and responsibilities the more conceptually, systemically you have to be able to think. You need to have a well-honed ability to see systemically how the parts interact as a whole.

Conceptualization is not a skill learned once you are at the executive level. It is a developmental skill that needs to be honed all along the way. The ability to see conceptually can be improved by holding a variety of positions and thereby broadening your entire conceptual spectrum of how business operates, taking on special interdepartmental assignments, and working with specific problems that you would not otherwise encounter in the course of your normal work, but which are necessary to broaden your thinking and skill.

So what if you are already a good conceptual thinker? In this case, you need to be helping others in your organization achieve this same level of competency. What did you do to learn this skill that might be of particular value to others? What assignments did you have that were particularly useful in helping you pull disparate parts of a system together to work more effectively? What projects, tasks or assignments do you need to seek out to aid development?

You'll be hard-pressed to find a senior-level leader that is still operating at the technical skills level. The higher you go the more you move away from the technical side of your business. Conversely, you'll find the best leaders have good systemic thinking and conceptual skills or if they recognize this as a weakness in their skill set, they have surrounded themselves with others who have this talent.

What is your level of conceptual thinking competency? Is your current mentor capable of helping you in this area? What assignments do you need to seek out that might help broaden your systemic and conceptual thinking abilities? If you already have a high competency in this area, whom do you need to be helping in your organization?

My Story

My first job in Corporate America was as a secretary. And because I was in the Training and Development Department and because I had been a teacher before taking this position, I was soon asked to facilitate the Secretarial Forum. This was a series of classes for newly hired secretaries to learn the particular methodology and procedures necessary for excellent business support. One of the session we always conducted was a Q&A with the General Manager's Executive Assistant. I remember very vividly a statement she made about skills being what were necessary to get a job and to be successful in the lower ranks, but the higher you advance the more relationships, networking and conceptual thinking become more important than actual job skills. I agree. The higher you go, the more responsibility you have the more you have to be able to think systemically and conceptualize rather than use actual job skills.

Teamwork: Basic Ingredients and Mercenary Tactics

Almost every CEO and manager I know is continually searching for how to bring together a great team. They are trying to create the right mix of competencies and personalities, make sure the environment is just right so everyone can excel and they are constantly monitoring the dynamic ebb and flow to ensure greatness. Chances are you, too, are searching for this magic elixir. The June 12, 2006 edition of *Fortune* magazine devoted almost the entire magazine to a series of articles on the 'Secrets of Greatness'. These *Fortune* articles address leadership and its various aspects from a wide variety of perspectives. I've extracted some of what I believe are the highlights into an executive summary below.

I give full credit to *Fortune* for spurring the idea to write about this topic, but the team tactics within professional bike racing they discuss I know first-hand having lived with the sport for many years. Cycling may not be your preferred sport or you may not even be a sports enthusiast, but I'll bet in the 10+ articles in this issue of *Fortune* you'll find both wisdom and wit.

Hallmarks of Teamwork

1. Clear definition of roles – you can't have collaboration if you have confusion among the members.

2. Small is good – the ideal team size is 4 to 6 members.

3. Outside threats – some stimulus causing urgency is required – often external to the organization.

4. It's a practice, an outcome – not something that can be willed. Like getting rich or falling in love, you can't cause it to happen, but you can create the conditions within which it can blossom.

5. Shared responsibility – you can't control others, but you can control yourself. Blaming others for failures is, by definition, a personal failure.

6. Establish norms and goals – when we take the time to establish norms and goals not only will groups behave accordingly, they will enforce rules on other group members. It's human nature. I've watched this as my granddaughter coaxed other kids back in line as they go out to the playground.

7. Group welfare, not incentives – life's richest experiences happen with others - no experiential activities in a team building session can cause teamwork to happen. But they can help create the atmosphere where group welfare and accomplishing goals through established norms is more sought after by the group.

Cutting Deals with the Enemy, Maximizing Liquidity, Punishing the Slackers - Sound like free-market enterprise? It's what goes on inside the peloton (the mass of cyclists in the main pack) of a professional cycling event. It sounds cut throat and it is. Winning is often brutal.

Many American's do not understand the strategy and tactics that occur in professional bicycle racing. Europeans are weaned on it. So we only take notice when one of our own is in the spotlight. But many who have watched Lance Armstrong may not understand what's going on and why. The race itself looks like a symphony of 150 whizzing, whirring wheels with an occasional sprint and crash sprinkled in for excitement. In fact, there are hundreds of small teams (yep, 4.6 or smaller) within the larger group of 150. Sound like the teams within your organization?

Cycling has an etiquette that all riders must honor or face being ostracized. Being ostracized in a bike race often looks like having to ride on your own with no help from others. You suffer the consequences by falling off the back quickly. This happens in business also when members don't understand the often unwritten rules. Friction erupts and attitudes change subtly. Cyclists deal with this head on and swiftly. Businesses often let these situations fester.

Within the moving mass of the peloton commodities are being exchanged almost constantly. What looks to be a rolling bike ride is really an "ordered, complex web of shifting alliances, in the midst of brutal competition, designed to keep or acquire the market's most valued currency". Sound like your business?

Cyclists conserve energy by riding in each others slipstream. As a result, enemies often stick together and make deals with each other. "Cooperation across enemy lines is the centerpiece of a winning game plan". While you have members of your own team in the peloton all working to get the strongest rider in position, doing so may mean you have to work a deal with the enemy. It is often necessary to make friends with enemies as quickly as you would make enemies of friends. Alliances are quickly made and remade all in the spirit of winning. (Quoted items were taken from the *Fortune* articles).

Case in point, in Stage 10 of the 2005 Tour de France, Lance Armstrong (USA) and his closest competitor, Ivan Basso (Italy), opened up a big gap on the rest of the field. They both had a common rival in Jan Ullrich (Germany). Lance turns to Ivan and strikes a deal. They work together to save energy by exchanging the lead and pulling each other along thus opening a larger gap between themselves and the main pack and together they extended the lead over Ullrich. Later in the Tour Lance catapulted past Basso, his one time friend, to win the individual time trial on Alpe d'Huez. Enemies can make common bed fellows when the circumstances call for it. It's not about friendship, it's about the business of winning.

Now let's relate cycling back to the Hallmarks of Teamwork.

1. Every rider has a clear definition of their role – team leader, sprinter, climber, domestique, etc.

2. Teams are small – 9 riders on each team, but often ride in smaller groups of 4-5 as others are carrying out their individual roles.

3. Outside threats are ever-present from all the other teams and individual strong riders. You have to be in the front in order to respond quickly when a move is made. Urgency is ever present.

4. It takes practice. You can't will yourself to be a winning cyclist. It takes hours and years in the saddle.

5. Shared responsibility – one person is in the limelight on the podium, but each member has a shared responsibility and shares in the glory of winning. If any member fails the team suffers; if the team doesn't support all riders, they all suffer. Prize money is shared among the team members so it is a win/win for all.

6. The goal is well established and discussed before each race – win the stage, win points at a critical point in the race, get TV coverage for sponsors, be in front as you roll through your home town, etc. Team meetings establish the goals before every stage and every race. Norms are strictly enforced in the peloton. You don't observe them, you'll be punished. No slackers allowed.

7. Group welfare is honored. Sure, they have the incentive of wanting to win, but if you don't take care of the team as a whole you don't have the opportunity to win.

There are may parallels between professional cycling and your business. After all both are business enterprises. It seems to me there are many lessons we can learn from watching the Tour de France or the Tour of California…or the Tour of Georgia…or the USA Pro Challenge in Colorado…and applying them to our own business lives.

My Story

No one reaches a successful position alone. We may often think we are the sole contributor to our success, but when we reflect we know many, many others had a hand in our ability to succeed. Early experiences in school, later on group assignments, participation in sports teams in college, work groups held accountable for results, and the support of family and colleagues all help us learn to be successful through using basic ingredients of team work and through the school of hard knocks of mercenary tactics.

There isn't enough space, time or paper to tell you of all those that have contributed to what success I've had, but suffice it to say it does take a village to make any one of us successful. Thank you to all who have had a hand in contributing to my success.

The Magic of Multiple Minds

Fall is the time of year we often think of getting our "act together" for the coming year. You know, making resolutions, setting our business plans in place, learning from and reflecting on this past year, etc. Each year I have the pleasure of creating my own strategic plan in collaboration with some of the brightest, most insightful, and caring business minds I know of.

I am a member of a Master Mind group which meets monthly. If you are too, you know how beneficial such a group can be. We are all business owners and we serve as a Board of Advisors for one another. Each year we escape to a wonderful mountain cabin set among pine trees overlooking a golf course that one of our members owns, so we have not only a beautiful location for our work, but the serenity and peacefulness adds to our productivity.

When you first start using a structured strategic planning process there is always a steep learning curve. So over the years all our Master Mind members have become well-versed in how to avoid the pitfalls the first year. And, sure enough, the plans we each produced this year are much more realistic, achievable and measurable than when we started this process several years ago.

But the magic does not happen just because we've been doing this for so long. The "magic" comes from how much better our plans are because we are able to honestly, openly, and candidly share our dreams and frustrations. Through our discussions we each end up with new insight into possibilities as well as practical methods of achieving our goals. Even though I have been facilitating and developing strategic plans for many years, my own company's plan is much richer because of the ability of others to see what I can't see and our ability to be honest and forthright with one another.

Here are some of the quoted benefits members are realizing:

- "Having a strategic plan and reviewing it monthly with each other really enhances personal accountability."

- "It is great to be able to share with others who understand and whose opinion you trust and value."

- "The methodology we use fits so well with my personal belief system – the synergy is terrific."

- "Our Master Mind group forced me to look at my strategic plan and review my progress at least once a month which was 12 times more frequently than I had ever thought of it before. Since I believe in the "law of attraction", this is a very positive force in my business."

- "Getting insight and affirmation from others who think differently than I do is very reassuring."

- "I've had the best year ever in my business partially because I had a plan and group accountability that kept me focused."

- "These business colleagues have become life-long friends who are willing and able to hold up the mirror which I often need to gaze into."

If you are a leader of a business or organization, I would highly recommend you consider starting a Master Mind group for yourself. If each of the member businesses does not already have a strategic plan, I would also highly recommend you consider establishing a group goal of each member business developing a strategic plan. You get what you focus on so what better way to achieve your business goals than to have a strategic business plan you focus on at least monthly. The sharing and discussion you get from business colleagues whose opinion you value is priceless.

My Story

This book is my story regarding this topic. I never would have created a collection of my various *TIPS* articles without the "Magic of Multiple Minds". My Master Mind group insisted there was a need, they insisted my words provided wisdom, and they nagged me into pulling it together. So there is truly magic in the multiple minds and thoughts that others share with us.

I do hope you find some wisdom in what I've shared. *TIPS* started out just being a way to stay connected with business colleagues, clients and potential clients in the intervening times when I wouldn't see them frequently. It blossomed into a frequently emailed column long before blogs were even thought of, and all those *TIPS* articles have matured into a book. May you find inspiration, motivation and joy in all my stories.

Your Best Mental Movies

My husband and I recently visited Tenerife in the Canary Islands. He conducted a triathlon training camp while I tagged along. The Canaries are known as the Hawaii of Europe and like their US namesake they are volcanic islands which you should interpret as meaning there is almost nothing flat on the island. So we spent a lot of time on our bicycles climbing slowly up very steep roads and descending very quickly. As we cycled I had flash backs to other times I've trudged up the mountains in the Rockies and the Alps. One thing that helps me stay focused, have the perseverance to keep putting one pedal in front of the other, and finally conquer the mountain is replaying mental movies.

Mental movies are those positive memories I store of other times I've done something equally challenging. I relive the smell of the meadow flowers, hearing the cow bells in the distance, seeing the mountain goats by the side of the road in the fog, feeling the sun on my back as the bees buzz around the flowers and before you know it, you have more miles behind you. The time and the miles go by much more easily and more quickly when I'm watching a movie. This is partly because I am suddenly some place else. It is also because I get a boost of energy, my muscles get a bit of virtual relief, pedaling becomes more even and stronger as I refocus, and my mind is more confident because I know I've "been there, done that before" successfully. When I act "as if" I am confident, full of energy, and believe I can conquer the mountain, I can. When I believe I am not able to, I can not. The mind and the body are one – one leads the other and in this case the body responds to the mental movies which are telling me I can do it…I can do it…I can do it and sure enough, I can and I do!

The key to being able to draw on your bank account of mental movies is to store only the best. TiVo them for future viewing. There is great value in storing memories of those times when you were successfully able to do something. While we learn from our mistakes, we learn more from our positive accomplishments.

I'm reminded of two quotes that underscore achieving tough goals. One is by Lance Armstrong who said something like… "motivation can't get you there if you don't have the legs, but if you have the legs and lack motivation, you're not going to get there". And the other is by a colleague, friend and very strong cyclist, Christina Maddox, who said something like, "You have to have commitment before you have passion. Passion follows commitment. The first step is to commit and then you have to have a great plan".

I'd add to these ideas one ingredient that can help your motivation and, as a result, increase your commitment and that is to bank the best of your mental movies and draw on them when you face tough challenges. Just like you TiVo your favorite broadcasts do the same with your personal bests. It doesn't make any difference what the situation happens to be. This technique helps whether you are climbing a physical mountain on your bicycle, climbing an emotional mountain in your life, or conquering a business challenge that seems insurmountable.

I'm watching this happen right now with my 8-year old granddaughter. She is learning to read more advanced books at the same time she is conquering more advanced gymnastics. As her confidence in the gym grows her ability to master more advanced reading is accelerating also. The mind and the body are one. One confidence breeds another and along the way she is filling her bank account with the best of her mental movies.

My Story

"I think I can, I think I can, I think I can," said the little train going up the mountain. This is a story I remember my mother reading to me when I was very small. It was the embryo of mental movies. Every time I tackle something I think is bigger than I am or is tougher than I think I can master, I relive "I think I can". I do this almost weekly when I ride a longer ride than I think I can do or I go up a steeper climb than I think I can concur. Thanks, Mom, I still think I can.

CHAPTER 3
Possibilities

Are Your Routines Stifling Your Possibilities?

Are your routines, the way you kind of go about your life on automatic pilot, helpful or hurtful? Are your patterns and habits getting you closer to your goals or not? We don't often think of habits as being an important part of goal setting or a critical part of achieving our objectives, but they are.

Don't get me wrong - I love routines. They are familiar, easy, often effective and sometimes pleasurable. But that may be precisely the problem. For the very same reasons, routines are also dangerously seductive. Undue reliance on them can cause you to become handcuffed, ultimately causing your todays and tomorrows to look like your yesterdays. Daily, well-trodden pathways can produce well-worn feelings. Be careful of routines, sometimes they are so good they are bad.

Of course, routines cannot be beaten when they help us accomplish recurring tasks; but if we want to construct wonderful memories, then we may need to halt what is ordinary and orderly in order to do what is extraordinary and new.

For many of us, our professional lives do us a favor. They provide variety and challenge. Even so, there is routine. We leave for work at about the same time each day, we travel the same route, we do similar tasks each day, we go home by the same route at about the same time, we eat, watch TV, check e-mail and voice mail, go to bed at the same general time, etc. And wake up the next day in order to do it all over again.

How about it? Will you remember today, tomorrow or the next day one year from now? If not, then maybe it's time to give yourself a break from your routine. Have an adventure. Make that call. Arrange that trip. Visit that place. Introduce yourself. Make a beginning. Make an ending. Write it. Buy it. Say it.

You work really hard all year in order to give gifts to other people at holiday time. Why not declare today a Personal Holiday and give yourself a gift. It's time to give yourself the gift of reassessment of your routines and habits with the willingness to get rid of those that aren't helping you and create new ones that give you possibilities.

My Story

We are all somewhat creatures of habit. It makes life so comfortable, predictable and easy. You just don't have to think about common things that occur frequently. I am this way too, but at the same time I love an adventure. I often will vary the route I take to do common chores just because I like the variety and adventure. I know I get this from my Dad as he was the same way. I know I can easily let routine stifle my possibilities and this is one reason why I intentionally seek to find new ways of doing ordinary things. It keeps my mind fresh, causes me to be more alert, and along the way I make new observations.

Benefits Emerge from Economic Challenges

Turn off the news!

With all the doom and gloom in the news today, it would be easy to believe there is nothing positive coming out of our current global economic situation. I am not belittling those many unfortunate situations in which people have been adversely affected. However, I, for one, and many of my friends and clients believe now is the time to look for and create positive opportunities.

It is easy to get caught up in what you hear on the news stations. Turn it off! And instead tune into all the good things that are going on around you. Opportunity abounds, but only if you are looking for it and decide to take advantage of it.

Get turned on to the good things around you!

I was reminded of this a couple of weeks ago when I was a guest speaker at a conference. At lunch I intentionally sat with people I had never met before. I turned to my left and introduced myself to the lady next to me. I inquired about how she had learned of the conference and where did she work. She replied, "Well, until this week I worked at Boeing, but I just got laid off". I replied that I was sorry to hear that and proceeded to engage her in further conversation. She replied, "Oh, I'm delighted I got laid off. It is just the push I needed to explore other interests and I'm confident things will turn out just fine." What a delightful, positive attitude. This woman was single so she wasn't relying on another person's income, yet she was very open to exploring and finding new opportunities.

Benefits of having been an employee!

Now is a time when many people choose to become entrepreneurs either because they are laid off and feel they must, or because they see an opportunity and take advantage of it. In these situations, take inventory of all the good things you learned to do and lessons you learned from your prior employers. I could write a book (Hum...now there's an idea...writing another book!) about the benefits I experienced from working in Fortune 500 companies for 30 years. I absolutely know I am a better business owner and consultant because of the training, experience and lessons I learned along the way during those years. I think those going into entrepreneurship now after having been an employee will find the same thing happening to them.

I believe we will look back 3 years, 5 years and 10 years from now and see positive changes that came out of this time period. Examples of how this has occurred in the past are:

- Nokia, which is now synonymous with cell phones, reinvented itself in the recession of the early 90's from being a paper, rubber and transmission cable company. Their goal was to sell 500,000 cell phones in 1994; they actually sold 20 million.

- Berkshire Hathaway, now synonymous with Warren Buffet, used to be a shirt maker in the heart of the textiles market in Massachusetts. As textiles waned, they got into insurance, aircraft and a variety of other industries.

- Apple Computers has grown from a stodgy minority computer company into the giant upstaging the more traditional Windows crowd. Their iPod eclipsed the Sony Walkman, iTunes revolutionized the retail music business, and iPads are the latest rage, etc.

- Google has taken over from AOL, Netscape and Yahoo and who knows where it will go next.

Refocus in order to grow!

From whom and from where will the next breakthrough come? From you? From your company? Rather than focusing on downsizing, cutting costs and laying off people, focus on what it would take to increase sales or launch that new opportunity which could grow your business rather than shrink it.

Raising capital and increasing capacity rather than struggling to cut costs and reduce investment in your company and your people is not only exciting, it is a positive growth strategy rather than a declining negative approach.

Remember, no one ever gained exponential prosperity from cost reduction. Prosperity always comes from possibilities.

My Story

I get so frustrated with the news. So much of it is negative and only rarely seems to be uplifting. I think George Bernard Shaw had it right in that the Pygmalion Effect can easily consume our lives and cause our prevailing attitudes and world view to be skewed. I naturally seek to find the glass half full so I get frustrated when what we see, hear and read about seems to take the half-empty approach. I'm looking at a glass of iced tea right now and it is more than half full. If I had already consumed more than half of it, I would see it only as an opportunity to get another refreshing glass full. For me, make mine positive news.

Casting Call for Personal Leadership

When the Oscar's are on TV, I typically don't watch them, but once in a while I hang in there until the last golden statue has been claimed. Watching the awards, it struck me that we each respond to casting calls every day. Which casting calls are you responding to?

We all face chosen and not chosen changes in our lives every day. As my friend Silver Rose (www.silverroseenterprises.com) says, "change is inevitable, but suffering is optional". Naturally, it is easier to be excited about changes we seek rather than those that seem to be thrust upon us. But even changes we choose often have negative impact on our lives. (OMG, will this child ever sleep through the night?...Housework! You mean Mom won't be cleaning the house now that I'm married?...You get a promotion, but it means you have to move...What! Leave my house and friends? You get the picture.)

When a change occurs which we didn't choose it is more difficult to embrace the change with a positive outlook, but even then there is a choice. How we accept the change and move on is totally in our control.

You lose your job...do you stay in your PJs until 10 or do you get up, dress "as if" you were going to work and embrace the day? You may have been out of the job market for quite a while...do you mope about or are you actively engaged in creating a network of business colleagues? Your employer is closing a division and you have a choice – move or find other work...are you stuck in the time-warp of your home and friends where you are or are you embracing the possibilities of a new location and new friends along with the growth and development they offer.

As my friend Silver reminds us, no matter the reason for the change, your reaction is totally up to you. Change is inevitable, sometimes welcomed and sometimes not, but in any case how we choose to respond is always our choice.

How are you responding to the changes in your life? How can you manage most effectively the challenges of these changes in order to capture the opportunity being offered to you? One window always opens when one gets closed. What windows of opportunity are you facing?

My Story

Every once in a while I go through some sort of change that seems all-consuming at the time. I get grumpy, the fuse on my temper seems to be shorter than normal, and I become more emotional. I know intellectually what is happening, but that doesn't make it any easier to tolerate the change I am living through at the time. I know these are times when I have to be even more aware of what is going on and my reaction to it.

Most recently this has been happening because we sold our Colorado home and were in temporary housing for a month; then we moved into our son's home while he and his wife were vacationing in Italy; and then we returned to our home in Arizona. Did I mention I've been going through a bit of change recently? It is times like these I am reminded to step up to my own personal leadership of managing change with my attitude consciously and intentionally staying positive.

Don't' Let Katrina Hit Your Organization

A very wise Japanese proverb says that "Vision without action is a daydream. Action without vision is a nightmare." A twist on this proverb could be "Averting a disaster without a plan is a daydream. Disaster without a plan is a nightmare". Recently, we've seen how true this is in a number of natural, world-wide disasters. Fires, tornadoes, tsunamis, floods, terrorist attacks, etc.

So what would your organization be like if a disaster struck? Just picture the confusion, mess, and frustration, not to mention the loss of productivity and business. We know we have the equivalent of weak levees, old worn out pumps, rusted pipes that will break, but what are we doing about it? We all get caught thinking "that was someplace else…it will never happen here". But are you aware of and are you planning for another type of major impact on your business that is coming more subtly, but no less disastrously than Katrina?

I'm speaking of the impact on your business of the retirement of the Baby Boomer generation. The US has a co-dependent relationship on this generation – we're all banking on our 401K's and other government and IRS-sanctioned retirement programs while the economy is banking on our continued spending. The fact that many of this generation will be retiring means change in a big way for every organization - and yours is no exception. Consider this series of questions and just imagine the preparation you need to be doing now.

> How many of your senior leaders will be retiring in the next 5 years?

> How many individual contributors in critical roles will be leaving you soon?

> Are the sales people who really drive your revenue in this generation?

> Do you have a leadership development plan which identifies and grooms the next generation of leaders?

> Are the skills you need to develop in your next generation of emerging leaders quick and easy to master or do you need to plan for a long development period or on making strategic hires?

> If you need to make strategic hires, where is this talent? Do you know where to find these individuals and what it will take to hire the skill sets and talent you will have to replace?

> Do you have a robust, complete, up-to-date set of policies, procedures, and practices in place so that new leaders coming in know "how things get done here" and so continuity of service won't be lost in the process?

> To what degree will your product and service development suffer as this generation of expertise leaves your organization?

> Have you planned ahead for the impact on your financial position to provide the retiree benefits your organization offers?

> Are you prepared if those in key positions are suddenly out for an unplanned extended period of time? Do you have a back-up plan? Are those in back-up positions prepared?

> And the big one: what if the person who will be retiring is the owner, President, GM, CEO or YOU. Do you have a succession plan and, if so, are you using the plan you have to replace the top person?

Hopefully, you have a solid answer for every one of these questions. Well-run organizations do. My point is not to scare you, but to prompt action if you aren't already well prepared.

Just like the Katrina scenario, the Army Corp of Engineers knew the levees were weak, the City of New Orleans knew it didn't have an adequate disaster plan, considerable investigation had been done following 9/11 about disaster preparedness, but plans and the ability to execute them were not in place. Don't let your organization get caught in the "disaster without a plan is a nightmare" situation. What actions do you need to take now?

My Story

Earlier in my career, keeping Katrina from hitting me looked like always focusing on my next career move, my next set of skills development, my next assignment, the next phase of my family's growth, my son's needs, etc.

In the past few years I've had to keep Katrina from hitting me in a very personal way. First, my mother passed away and because my sister and I had been proactive, her estate was relatively easy to manage, although there always seem to be details that are unexpected.

Now I am personally in the midst of slowing down my own business so I am cleaning out files, transferring records to data storage for safe keeping, mentoring a protégé, and deciding how I want to use my time in a different, yet productive way.

So no matter what stage of life we are in, we have to both personally and professionally plan for weathering whatever storm might unexpectedly come along.

In Praise of Others

This article in on the great work and good news three firms I'm working with are accomplishing. Don't get me wrong – their growth, success and leadership is not due to my counsel nearly as much as it due to their dedication, hard work, and personal leadership. Here's to each of you for your caring and pursuit of excellence on behalf of your employees, your companies, and your stakeholders.

Really listening to your employees – Most companies will say their most important asset is their employee base, but just try to get a good Wall Street rating on that basis. We know it's true, but Wall Street tends not to put it into a financial equation. I take my hat is off to one of my clients who is truly listening to his employees.

This company recently conducted an employee survey – you know the typical "what do you like, what could be better around here" kind of questions. It takes courage to conduct an employee survey. After all, it implies willingness to listen to your most important customer…your employees. What is atypical is that they are listening and doing something about what they heard. To quote this leader, "Since the need for strong leadership was one of the primary areas addressed in the employee comments, we're in the midst of working together to create the type of leadership behaviors and norms needed to take this company where it needs to go in the future". Congrats on having the courage to listen <u>and act</u>. Most companies go through the motions, but don't take any real action.

Keeping Score – It's relatively easy to create a strategic plan although many companies don't do it. It's another thing altogether, however, to score your results monthly against objective, quantifiable measures, discuss the results openly, share the results with the entire staff, and keep the "scorecard" visible. That's exactly what one of my clients is doing and they are absolutely convinced (and so am I) that keeping score, talking about what's working and what's not, and keeping the focus on their targets will significantly increase their ability to achieve results. They are 3 months into their fiscal year and not on target to achieve their goals – if they didn't have objective measures in place and a monthly discussion of them they wouldn't be able to make mid-course adjustments reallocating resources as needed to meet goals. They will get on track because 1) they want to be successful and 2) they have a mechanism for knowing how much they are behind and against which specific goals they need to take more aggressive action.

Remodeling, redesigning and reassigning – You know what a chore living through remodeling can be – the confusion, the mess, the constant need to clean up and live through the process. Imagine doing that at the same time you're redesigning the work units and, as a result, reassigning some of the employees to different work cells all while you meet production goals, not lose sight of quality, and get through year end activities. There is never a good time to take a business through this type of transition. It's a tall order for a leader to tackle. But when you're literally busting at the seams and have to expand to meet demand this is exactly what you have to do. The "rest of the story" is the newly remodeled space is clean, beautiful, bright, roomy enough to really be productive, and the pride on everyone's face is showing. This transition means big time change for everyone and well-managed change starts with effective, proactive, highly involved leadership.

Leading the Change

- ✓ Be the example you're trying to create.

- ✓ Making tough decisions.

- ✓ Adjust as you go.

- ✓ Encourage everyone along the way.

- ✓ Celebrate Success.

These are the key elements of leading change successfully and all three of these companies are working diligently to be excellent examples. How well are you managing change at your company? What can you learn from these stories that will help you surpass the challenges you are facing?

My Story

The most wonderful part of my professional life has been the opportunity to in some small way help individuals and organizations grow and achieve results beyond what they thought they could achieve. My pleasure comes in seeing the results, watching the pride swell in the hearts of those who worked so hard for those achievements, and seeing individual growth take place. My greatest reward is getting to sing the praises of others. Thank you to all my clients who have allowed me to be a participant in your journey.

Learning from Our Athletes

It seems everywhere you look these days you can see incredible feats under extreme conditions. Unfortunately, often we don't really see them or learn from them because we get caught in the daily trap of activity. Just picture the Olympics, the Tour de France, the US Tennis Championships, the Ryder Cup, the NBA All-Stars. In all these activities you see tremendous perseverance to overcome adversity and outstanding examples of leadership.

Watching and Learning

Over the years, we have all watched hours of the Olympics and I had the extremely good fortune to be able to attend Tour de France cycling road race? While we admire and marvel at the skill, dedication and courage of these athletes from around the world, I remain in awe of the 192 cyclists who every year grind out 2,100+ miles of cycling in the searing heat, cold rain, extremely steep climbs and plunging descents day after day (not to mention setting on a bike for hours on end day after day!). I do get caught up in the excitement and enthusiasm of the event, but the real gem is in reliving and learning from the experience. In addition to our amazement at the athletic skill of our idols, what can we learn from their examples?

- ✓ Faithfully following a plan yields results.

- ✓ Few great gains are made without sacrifices.

- ✓ If the goal is worthy enough, the dedication is worth the effort.

- ✓ Despite unexpected obstacles don't lose sight of the goal.

- ✓ There are no quick fixes or easy routes to high goals.

- ✓ Sweet rewards stay with you forever.

- ✓ And on and on and on….

In my work, I help organizations achieve goals which often seem just as difficult and unattainable as a gold medal or a podium finish. But through effectively managing change, diligently following a strategy, measuring progress, living the example you want to create, and an insatiable drive to excel, you and your business will also be on the podium and receive the acclaim you seek and deserve. Common to both business and athletics are:

- ✓ Unyielding willingness to plan and prepare.

- ✓ Clarity about purpose and priorities.

- ✓ Long-term dedication.

- ✓ Support all along the way.

- ✓ Celebration of success.

What can you learn and apply from the heroics you've seen recently? How can your hero's or heroine's spur you on to the greatness you are seeking for your business and in your personal life? How will you apply what you've learned?

My Story

My life has been enriched many fold because of the athletic pursuits of my family. I'm the want-to-be and they are the true athletes. My husband went through college on two athletic scholarships, our son was a professional bicycle racer competing in Europe for many years and then in the US. They were the jocks and I was the pretend. But because I have a competitive spirit even though I am not a natural born athlete, I joined right in and ended up doing OK for myself.

I know I became a more perseverant and tolerant person and, therefore, a more understanding and patient consultant because of my competitive athletic pursuits. Thank you, Joe and Dirk, for setting the way and to all the other athletes I have admired and learned from as I cheered you on from the sidelines.

Lemonade and Purposeful Living

We have all at one time or another had to live through the computer problems from the Nether World. You know those times when everything seems to crash, you back up files, but not as recently as you should have, and of course, you're facing a deadline at the time. In the midst of a computer saga recently I was reminded of my purpose and the mission of my company which is to continually build skill and capability and guide people and organizations toward their optimal success and performance.

At one point in the middle of this tangled computer nightmare, I was on hold with Tom, a particularly helpful and very pleasant young man in customer service at my email and web service provider. We struck up a conversation as their system transferred my web site files. I took this opportunity to make lemonade even though I felt like I and my computer were buried in a truck load of lemons. Tom was having difficulty figuring out what he wanted his college major to be so he quit school for a while to earn some money and sort things out. The problem is all he was doing was working and not sorting things out. Sound familiar to you?

So as we waited and talked I asked him a series of questions which you'll recognize as my attempt to lead Tom toward more purposeful living. Things like...

- ✓ What did he want to be doing 5 years from now? (He had no idea. Do you?)

- ✓ What did he enjoy and not enjoy about the courses he had taken?

- ✓ Did he enjoy his work? Was it satisfying enough to be his life's work? If not, what was he doing currently to get himself back on track and back in school?

- ✓ Who could he interview, talk with or shadow in order to learn more about potential careers he is considering?

- ✓ Had he inquired about what tuition aid and school benefits his current employer provided?

- ✓ Did he intend to go to school full-time or could he work part-time and take a few classes while he worked?

- ✓ He told me he had been a summer intern in a law firm and decided not to become an attorney based on that experience. Why? What didn't he like about that profession and was there a way to identify a profession that captured what he did enjoy during his internship?

By the time my files were transferred he was enthusiastic about getting focused on sorting out what career area he might want to pursue and getting back into school. And I was feeling better about that truck load of lemons and the sweet taste of lemonade.

I share this story because it demonstrates how we all need to find the lemonade among the lemons. Also, no matter how frustrating life might become or how complicated seemingly simple tasks turn out to be, we can find ways to live and extend our life's purpose in the midst of the circumstances. It also is a great reminder that we all need to focus on where we want to be 5 years from now and make concrete decisions about what we are going to do now to get ourselves one step closer to those goals.

My Story

What can I say? I'm a committed optimist. And because I see my life's purpose as helping others grow and go beyond where they are it is second natural for me to have a conversation like the one I cited above with a complete stranger over the phone.

I've always said that if we knew by age 40 what our major in college should have been we were doing well. This certainly applies to me. My undergrad was a double major in Social Studies and Physical Education. I was a teacher for a few years before stumbling into the profession I should have been in all along. I was fortunate to have a series of positions which led me to Organizational Development and eventually a Masters degree in this area. Too bad I didn't know about this field of study when I was 20, but then, when I was 20 girls became teachers. The rest is history...or rather mystory.

Lessons from The Devil

Power, politics and influence in organizations is an area I have helped individuals and organizations with over the years. I recently rewatched the movie "The Devil Wears Prada" with friends and was delighted to find so many powerful lessons in the movie. It isn't just that Meryl Streep is both a devilishly wicked boss while being a fashion icon for those of us in the "more mature" generation, it is packed full of lessons about the use and abuse of power, politics and influence. It is funny, poignant and full of life lessons. If you haven't watched it, do so.

<u>Women</u> – you'll love it, be able to relate directly to it, and wish you were as thin and willowy as some of the actresses and as beguiling as Meryl while clearly identifying with the tough choices the co-star (Ann Hathaway) has to make…

…career versus relationship.

…taking a job which is not what you think you want, but is clearly a stepping stone to what you dream of.

…tackling assignments which you think are impossible and succeeding.

…thinking you can't and finding out you can.

…and on and on and on throughout the movie.

<u>Men</u> – you'll need to put on a different set of lenses. Meryl is a king pin in a man's world. You'll see some tough lessons about the persona women sometimes believe they have to (and in fact often do have to) take to "make it" in a man's world. Many see the women's fashion industry as "female", but it is really very cutthroat and brutal and in many respects not "pretty" at all.

…sure it's a man's world in many regards, but men also wrestle with the same career versus relationship dilemmas that are depicted in the movie.

…I'm sure every male colleague I have can tell me about taking less-desirable positions in order to get to the more desirable position of their dreams.

…men learn some of the tough lessons earlier in life than women do due to their upbringing, but it doesn't make the lessons any less painful to learn.

…I'll bet men have a lot of self-doubt at times (and get darn frustrated at times because societal pressures cause them to keep their feelings hidden) but soon learn they are capable of doing more than they thought they could.

…and on and on and on throughout the movie.

So you see, 'The Devil Wears Prada', may also be "The Devil Wears Savile Row". There are a host of lessons to be found in this blockbuster movie. Women, I challenge you to see the movie (or see it again!) and look for the lessons this time rather than the fashion. Men, I challenge you to get in touch with your feminine side and rent it also. As you watch it, relate to and be tolerant and supportive of the often tough choices your wife, daughter, daughter-in-law, sister and female colleagues face.

My Story

In 1974 I had the privilege of meeting Billi Lee (www.thesavvyinstitute.com). She is a dynamo who has spent a lifetime helping others understand and learn to play the game of power and politics successfully. I must have had one aha moment per minute during her 3-hour presentation. You see I was young, new to the corporate world, very naïve, and simply hadn't been around that block before.   I've kept contact with Billi and relish the opportunity to know her now as a friend as well as a business colleague.

At one point in my career, I taught a graduate school level course in Power and Politics in Organizations. It is amazing how freeing it is when you learn the rules, begin to see the game being played, and learn to play the game well yourself. Oh yes, there are rules, you are playing a game, and you can learn to play it successfully. Seeing the corporate world this way allows you to release the tension, some of the concern, and put into perspective the mystery you feel you've been living in. You still have to work hard at playing the game, but gamesmanship can be fun as well as rewarding.

In my case, I not only released a lot of tension, I began to advance more quickly when I learned the rules of the game.

Passion and Purpose Lead to Prosperity

It's a chicken and egg kind of puzzle – which comes first, the passion or the purpose? Does your passion lead to your purpose or do you find your purpose because of what you are passionate about? I'm sure we could debate this for a long time and probably both arguments are right to some degree, but in the long run it doesn't make any difference. The bottom line is your results will soar when you have your purpose and passion aligned.

What would happen if you decided to focus your time, talent and energy on what you love to do? Do you think your results would improve? Would you be happier? Would your quality of life improve? What if what you do for a living wasn't work but you got paid to do what you love to do? Hopefully you are thinking, "She is describing what I am doing right now. I am doing what I love to do and getting paid to do it." My hope is that you are, in fact, thinking that right now.

I had the pleasure and good fortune to be able to travel to Singapore and Thailand. My husband was asked by a very entrepreneurial and wonderfully talented young business owner to meet with groups of triathletes in both Singapore and in Phuket, Thailand. Joe conducted both lecture format and hands-on clinics for these athletes. As I watched the participants interact, I saw a mirror image of my belief system and what I try (with passion I might add) to instill and provide to my clients. Passion, purpose and, in turn, greater prosperity.

Each of these participants came because they were:

➢ <u>Dedicated</u> to improving their performance.

➢ <u>Willing to invest</u> in learning and growth in order to excel.

➢ <u>Improving</u> their quality of life by surrounding themselves with the support of others from whom they learn and give back to in return.

➢ <u>Focused</u> on a vision of what they can achieve and have a plan for how to go about achieving it.

➢ <u>Living the life</u> they love and loving the life they live.

Whether or not these athletes end up on the podium or not, they will be winners because their passion and purpose will yield prosperity in the form of improved results and athletic performance.

So if you are not one of those people who loves the life you are living you might start by answering some of these questions and through self-examination decide how you can move closer to living the life you love.

➢ What are you passionate about?

➢ If you could do it for free and still have the lifestyle you want, what would you be doing?

➢ When you have free time or leisure time, what do you think about, what occupies your dreams?

➢ What aspects of your life do you enjoy?

➢ How can you integrate more of what you enjoy doing into your life now?

➢ What are you doing now that really doesn't require your skills, talents, time?

➢ What could you hire done by someone else so you could have more time for what you love and want to be doing?

➢ Life is about choices and trade-offs, what are you willing to stop doing or give up in order to get more of what you want?

OK, no one said the answers to these questions would be easy, but again it is a trade-off. Are you willing to put a bit of thought and effort into getting closer to what you love or are you content to continue in your current path? One thing is for sure – you get what you focus on so if you focus on what you love and the things required of you to get closer to living the life you love, you'll get closer to it. Whether you love the life you are living right now or choose to pursue other options make sure you enjoy the journey for in the end the journey will be your memories.

My Story

I was fortunate to discover my passion about 25 years ago. Some people never seem to identify what they are passionate about. In my case, I was taking a leadership development and personal growth workshop provided for all the senior leaders in our company. It was conducted by a group called the Pecos River Learning Center from Pecos River, New Mexico.

One of the exercises was to write as precisely and concisely as possible a statement of our life's purpose and also to declare what we were passionate about. Until that moment, I hadn't given this topic much thought. I knew what I was good at, I knew what I liked to do, I knew what I was finding success in doing, but I hadn't actually written down my purpose and my passion. This simple request isn't necessarily easy to fulfil, but it is a powerful exercise I would encourage you to do if you haven't already done so. For me my passion and purpose became solidified. I could begin to zero in on specific tasks, jobs, and positions that would help me develop my abilities in these areas more fully. And as a result, I began to grow exponentially in my profession. After all, we get what we focus on, but how can we know what to focus on precisely if we haven't identified our passion and purpose.

The tag line for my company is "Where Passion Meets Performance" and that just about sums it up. I am passionate about helping individuals and organizations grow and go beyond where they otherwise would have been.

Personal Power to Change Results

Set a goal and you achieve it. Keep wishing for something and you are able to get it. Think negative thoughts and bad things happen. Think positive thoughts and good things happen. Ever wonder why?

I know from my own experience and the experiences of my clients that having a well-thought out strategy with quantifiable measures which you actively use to guide your life and business increases the probability of improved results. I also know if you don't have a strategy you'll go wherever life takes you and it may not be where you want to go. So what gives goal setting and mental messages such power?

Napoleon Hill wrote about the Law of Success pointing out that some of the key ingredients are self-control, enthusiasm, commitment to self and belief in possibilities. It is these same ingredients that make goal setting and mental messages so powerful.

If the CD or DVD in your mind constantly plays positive messages about possibilities for achieving your goals, your chances of success are significantly improved because you begin to see all sorts of opportunities for fulfilling those goals. Likewise, if the mental playlist you listen to plays only negative tunes and is filled with doom and gloom you will only see barriers to your goals.

We each have the personal power to change the results we are getting because we each have the personal power to determine what we want to think and, therefore, what we are likely to achieve. If we don't have influence and power over ourselves, then who can we influence? Getting what we want, succeeding rather than failing starts with a self-commitment to influence ourselves positively in order to fill our lives with possibilities and potential.

Changing our results starts with our own mental messages which are based on our belief system. My belief system is that we all have choices and that we each have to be accountable for owning our own choices. I may not like the choices others make that have adverse impact on me, but I do have choice about how I react, the mental messages I tell myself about the circumstances, and the power to influence and change my own actions as a result.

Maybe now is a good time to do a bit of self-assessment. What is the mental playlist you've been listening to lately? Is it affirming or disaffirming what you want in your life? What do you feel you have little control over that, in fact, you can begin to influence just by how you choose to think about it? Are you willing to try to change how you think about your goals and what you want or does your belief system tell you others are in control of your thoughts?

My Story

For several years, I've had a ritual I do every year on New Year's Day. It's a time to look forward and to reflect on the past year. So while I'm waking up from the party the night before, listening with one ear to the parade's on the TV and waiting for the football games to start, I set down with a pen and pad of paper and lay out my goals for the year. I segment these into personal and professional, learning/growth and financial, physical and lifestyle categories.

Because I've been doing this for several years, I have a repository to build on. Each year when I reflect, I am delighted with the number of goals I achieve. They often don't take a lot of work on a continual basis, yet I am pleasantly surprised at the progress I've made. We do get what we focus on so when we put energy into the environment we tend to gravitate toward it, and particularly when we share our goals with others, we achieve them. Writing down goals and sharing them with others establishes a basis for accountability. And if you are a determined person like I am, setting a goal automatically creates incentive to achieve it. We naturally don't want to fail others and we certainly don't want to fail ourselves.

Strategic Thinking

Have you ever thought about thinking? Sounds kind of like a trick question, but I am not intending it to be. I often find myself thinking about how people think. In my profession, you have to be a bit of a psychologist ...always looking for the reason behind why people do what they do. As a result, I frequently need to figure out the rationale for peoples' behaviors.

One of the ways I can be most beneficial to my clients is to help them understand the logic of their own and other peoples' actions. People always do what they do because of what happens to them when they do it. This simple statement is profound and absolutely true in any situation. It may not seem logical from your perspective, but from their point of view what they do always makes sense to them.

If you are in a leadership position, learning how to think strategically as well as tactically is critical. Tactical thinking is all about how to get the near-term and more immediate tasks completed. It is the tactics of the day-to-day operation. At the same time, because of your leadership role, you have to continually be thinking strategically. What's the bigger picture, what should today's actions and decisions be in order to be positioned for the future, etc.

There is a pattern of strategic thinking which some use without even thinking consciously about it. For others, learning to think strategically would be very beneficial. If you find yourself in situations where you know how to proceed in the near-term, but have a tendency to not check your actions as compared to your future needs and goals, this pattern will be useful to you. Thinking strategically means you...

✓ <u>Decide where you have to go</u>, where you have to be at X point in the future, what your goal is.

✓ <u>Identify issues</u> that will be both beneficial and potentially harmful in achieving that goal.

✓ <u>Determine the options</u> available to you to build upon the benefits identified and avoid the obstacles.

✓ <u>Create a plan</u> from these options that optimizes the benefits and minimizes the risks with the longer-term goal in mind.

✓ <u>Implement the plan</u>...here is where the tactical actions come back into play.

I find people in leadership positions tend to naturally think strategically, but if this isn't your natural pattern you can learn to do so by following the steps above. Where the challenge comes in for most every leader is in the last step...execution of the strategy. The overwhelming tendency is to get caught up in tactical day-to-day activities causing the strategic, bigger picture focus to become fuzzy. Intellectually it is understood, but on a practical level it gets lost in the crush of activity.

Taking this quick Strategic Quotient quiz will help you analyze your own thinking and pinpoint where you might need to improve this aspect of your leadership ability. Answer yes or no to each of these questions:

___1.   Do you have a well-articulated, clearly stated strategy that pinpoints goals with quantifiable measures for gauging progress?

___2.   Could you write a one or two sentence statement of that strategy?

___3.   Could each of your subordinates write a one or two sentence statement of that strategy without consulting each other?

___4.   Do you use this strategy as a guide in making important business decisions?

___5.   Have you as a management team tried to obtain consensus about the future of your firm?

___6.   Did you get consensus or are there still different visions of what your organization is trying to become?

___7.   Is recognition and reward for you and others based upon short-term or long-term goals? If both, what is the ratio of long-term to short-term recognition?

___8.   Are you and your subordinates recognized and rewarded for making wise long-term decisions?

___9.   Are the measures of success for personal and company performance aligned with your strategic objectives?

If all your answers are positive, then you are in good shape. The greater the number of negative answers and the wider the discrepancies between your responses and those of your subordinates, the more you need to work on strategically thinking personally and in leading your organization as a strategic thinker.

If you find your numbers indicate you need to become a more thorough strategic thinker, begin by trying to state to yourself what the goals, mission and objectives of your company are. If you can't state them clearly yourself, you can't expect your followers to be able to do so. Then begin to craft time-oriented goals with quantifiable measures attached to them. Ultimately, you want to share the goals, objectives and measures with all employees.

We all can easily stay in the activity trap, but leadership is about keeping the needs of today in perspective with the goals of tomorrow. You need to lead, but others need to follow and together you need to arrive where the company needs to be. It is extremely difficult to do this without a plan for the journey.

My Story

Some things come naturally. For me thinking in big pictures, strategy, seeing the parts as well as the whole, seems to come naturally. It's just the way I'm wired. I'm sure this is a big part of the reason I gravitated to my profession because I need to be able to see the whole and yet analyze the parts to help others identify concerns, create a plan for closing gaps, and develop solutions along the way.

I remember as a child taking this role with my cousins as we'd try to figure how to how get something we wanted from our grandparents. What do we want? What were the objections our grandparents might point out? What did we have to do to overcome those obstacles? How could we position our request so it was something they would want us to have?

As children we knew we were manipulating and scheming to get what we wanted. As adults we become a bit more sophisticated and change our approach to be more tactful, but in the end the higher you rise in an organization, the more responsibility you have, the more you have to be a good strategic thinker.

Taking the Leap - Leaving Corporate America

I often say, "The toughest decision I ever had to make in business was the decision to leave IBM". Yes, amazing as it might seem, it was gut-wrenching to decide to leave that treadmill, corporate maze, bastion of blue. This is incredulous to those who are still on the treadmill, feel trapped and don't know where the "stop" button is located. My next sentence is almost always, "But I'm better able to serve you as an advisor and consultant because of it".

The topic of this article is about learning from our own decisions and folding that back into how we help others.

The Background – Life after Eastman Kodak Company (EKC)

After 27 years at EKC, I landed what was my dream job. I was at a senior level, with world travel, working with high-profile clientele, my colleagues were respected and seasoned, and a world-renown company wanted me. It was the position I aspired to and prepared for my whole career and I got it. What more could I ask for? What could possibly be wrong? Why didn't everything seem right?

The Reflection - Be careful what you ask for because you just might get it…and I did.

In this case, I got to the top of the mountain and didn't like the view. Then I had to figure out why and learn to deal with it.

I had never been in a position before where life was so out-of-balance. I'm sure I was fortunate to have gotten to early retirement age and just now be learning this tough lesson, but no matter what your age when it hits you, it is disorienting, disheartening and dizzying. Life felt like a fog.

One of my specialties is helping organizations and individuals learn to lead and deal with change effectively and here I was in the midst of it. I knew all about the psychological, physiological, and behavioral effects of change from an intellectual perspective. What I was experiencing first-hand was the emotional impact of significant change (career change, demotion/ promotion, divorce/marriage, birth/death, moving, retirement, severe illnesses, etc.). Having "been there and done that" is precisely why I am now better prepared to help my clients with their own change management challenges.

The Learning - Here are some of the things I learned through this experience.

➢ **Stepping outside** - It is really difficult to step outside the circumstances and view logically what is happening emotionally. Don't be afraid to rely on friends, family and other experts in the field to help you see more clearly. When you are in the fog it is hard to see the sun shining someplace else nearby.

➢ **Being alone** - Because your whole world seems out of focus and the imbalance seems so totally consuming, you feel like you are the only person in the world who is going through this. Realize that everyone who is experiencing significant change is riding the same roller coaster. While we all move through the maze at different rates, no one escapes it.

➢ **Keeping it in** - You feel so incapable of expressing your confused state that you tend to bottle it up. Find a colleague, friend or family member and just start talking about it. It is amazing how just talking and someone listening can bring focus to the situation and through the process you often decide what action to take and have the courage to take it. If you are the friend or family member listening, there is no need to find a solution. The speaker isn't looking for one necessarily. Just listen and be respectful of their feelings. Your attentiveness alone often helps them find their own solution and way out of the fog.

➢ **Finding the light at the end of the foggy tunnel** – It feels like you'll never be able to get life back in order again. Well, for the people who don't "talk it out", turn to others for help, and analyze what is really going on they may get trapped in the maze. But for most of us, if we do the first three things I've mentioned above and give ourselves some time, we do emerge from the maze stronger and more mature.

➢ **Continue the learning** – I find myself frequently reliving this situation. I'll bet if you have been through a significant change, you do too. And we're better for it. Distance and time help us see the situation even more clearly so keep the learning going.

My Story

Well this article, in essence, is my story, but to position this as Paul Harvey would with the rest of the story…of course, the saga continues. Not a day goes by as a business owner that I don't continue to use the skills, experiences and knowledge I gained in the first 30 years of my professional life. Every client I've ever had in one way or another is managing change. So the saga continues as I perpetually help them understand, learn to manage and lead change effectively. As the saying goes, some things never change…death…taxes…and the fact there will be more change ahead.

The Best Don't Manage

We all are continually seeking to be the best at leading, managing, owning, developing, etc. Just note the huge sale of books such as *Good to Great, Developing the Leader Within, The Leadership Challenge, Built to Last,* and on and on and on. While these books very effectively point out examples to follow and practices to emulate, there is just nothing quite as powerful as experiencing greatness first hand. The case in point below demonstrates how "the best don't manage".

Over the years I have worked with hundreds of CEOs, Presidents, and owners, some of whom were very effective and all genuinely and sincerely were trying their best. Once in a while you come across someone who possesses a personal belief about the goodness in people and has a personal style that allows their belief to permeate through all they do. As a result those around them accept challenges beyond their expected horizon and truly blossom into a heightened level of their own potential.

I have a client who fits this description. I'd like to share with you some of the traits that allow this person to maximize the best in others by very subtly "managing" not only their own behaviors but all the activities of their company. Seldom do they have to overtly "manage" people or processes, they surround themselves with people who have potential and then allow that potential to grow.

Here are some examples of what they do and how they do it. They realize…

- The critical importance of hiring the right people – better to do without than hire the wrong person.

- If an employee can't be inspired, they made a mistake in hiring them and both the employee and the organization at-large will be better served the sooner this employee is gone.

- That even if it is difficult to do sometimes you have to "de-hire" a person who just doesn't fit and never will. Yes, this does happen even when you are doing your best to follow the statement above.

- For the most part, employees really do know what they are doing, the key is to get out of their way and let them do it.

- Accountability and consequences (both positive and negative) must be used hand-in-hand for empowerment and human potential to grow. They use positive reinforcement at least four times more frequently than negative reinforcement to create an enriching, positive culture where results can flourish.

- Trust must first be given away before you get it back in return so they willingly give the benefit of the doubt until proven otherwise.

While this client spends a lot of time thinking about and subtly positioning his own behavior and that of others in order to get the results that are needed, he does very little overt "managing" of people and processes because the employees have willingly stepped up to the challenge. His role is to set the direction, chart the course, keep the organization on task at a high level, ensure accountability is in place, provide liberal positive consequences for work well done and not hesitate to take corrective action when warranted. As a result he seldom has to step into a more demanding "manager" role that is so typically stereotyped. He spends a lot of time listening, asking questions, helping, thinking and smiling.

I recently facilitated a senior leadership team work session for this organization. And, while I didn't actually keep track of the amount of time this person talked versus the air time of his managers, I feel confident in saying he spoke less than 30% of the time. He set the tone, stated the objectives, asked questions, gave affirming answers and confirmed decisions others were making. This CEO is a delight to work with and I can only image how empowering, energizing, and engaging it is to work with him.

My Story

Some people make leading seem effortless. I know it isn't. I know they work really hard and are very intentional about their actions and behaviors, but they make it look easy. I believe this is somewhat due to the fact that they are comfortable in their own skin, they know themselves well, they know what they are about and they have a clarity of purpose. At least this has been my observation.

I've been very fortunate to have several of these kind of people as mentors. Some of them didn't know in a formal sense that they were mentoring me, but every one of them provided a wonderful example. So thank you Joe, Dirk, Bill, John, Chris, and Jim for being the example I needed at various times in my life.

Tough Choices

All too often in the news we hear only the events which cause our opinion of top business leaders to be diminished. Granted, leading any size corporation isn't easy and the lives of those at the top of the largest organizations are extremely public. In many ways this only serves to heighten the responsibility these leaders have not only to themselves and their corporations, but to the public at-large.

I recently read a book full of wisdom which I highly recommend. It is about life and leadership lessons. My copy is now messy with underlines, notes in the margins and dog-eared pages. *Tough Choices* by Carly Fiorina is a memoir of her life including her very public departure from HP. While I strongly advise you read the entire book, below I am sharing with you some of what I believe are the highlights. Enjoy!

LEADERSHIP

- <u>Character</u> is made up of <u>candor</u> (speaking the truth and speaking up and out), <u>integrity</u> (preserving your principles and acting on them), and <u>authenticity</u> (knowing what you believe, being who you are and standing up for both).

- Life is about the journey, not the destination. The steps along the way are what make us who we are.

- People like to be asked about themselves. This is a great management tool. You get smart fast by listening.

- A boss's confidence in an employee is a powerful motivator. When employees see you believe in their potential, they begin to look for it in themselves. Believing in someone else, so they can believe in themselves, is a small but hugely significant act of leadership.

- Each time I overcame my own fear, I was stronger. A leader's job is to help people overcome their fear.

- Live your life in a way that makes you happy and proud. If you sell your soul, no one can pay you back.

- Strategy should be ennobling. An organization's effort must be sustained through worthy purpose.

- Change can only begin if its force is greater than the weight of history and the power of the status quo.

ACCOUNTABILITY FOR CHOICES

- If we cannot choose our circumstances, we can always choose our response to them. If we cannot choose who we are, we can always choose to become something more. We cannot always choose the hurdles we must overcome, but we can choose how we overcome them. To stop choosing is to start dying. We can only be diminished if we choose to allow it.

- Value isn't measured by title or position, but by what someone is made of and how they choose to use it.

OFFICE POLITICS

- Office politics is based on power – who has it, who lost it, who wants it. You have to learn to play the game and see it as a game to be successful.

- Like it or not, seniority and familiarity can and do sometimes trump results. Looking and acting the part sometimes wins.

- Gender alone sometimes denies the presumption of competence. I had to work harder and be better prepared than anyone else to gain credibility. To do so I had to convince people I knew what I was talking about in the first few minutes. Only then would they listen to what I had to say.

PLAYING TO WIN

- If you can't play to win, you may as well not play.

- We did change goals because they turned out to be tougher than we anticipated. We did not think about how we might lose. We thought about how we could win. We won because we chose to.

- All triumphs are made of the same stuff: the right support, the right team, the determination to achieve the goal, lots of really hard work. Triumphs are much more about choices than about chance.

- People will always behave rationally based upon their own self-interest. They behave irrationally simply because they believe someone else is going to do so.

- If only one part or parameter of a complex problem is understood or acted upon, the problem cannot be solved. Only by comprehending the whole system – its interactions, dependencies, constraints and pressures – can a real, sustainable improvement be made.

My Story

I enjoy reading. It transports me to another place and time and in that journey I relax, de-stress and temporarily forget about trying to be a Super Mom, Super Grammy, Super Wife, Super Professional, etc. However, I can easily get caught up in reading fiction and neglect professional reading. So I have a reading rule. For every 2 or 3 fiction books I read, I read one professional book. My reading rule keeps me growing professionally and gives me a relaxing reward also.

Once in a while you run into a non-fiction book that is as equally engaging as the fictional stories I like to get absorbed in. *Tough Choices* was one of those books. I got very absorbed, could relate to the political situations, could draw analogies to choices I had faced, and developed a much deeper understanding of the circumstances leaders at the top face. Whether you like the eventual outcome of Carly Fiorina's tenure at HP or not, reading this book certainly will increase your admiration for her personal leadership convictions and decisions.

Transformation – One Pound at a Time

You know the old saying, "The way you eat an elephant is one bite at a time". Well, the same is true of how you lose weight – one pound at a time. I have been up and down in my weight twice in my life. This most recent time…and last time I might add…I lost 55 pounds over 4 months due to lots of exercise and sensible eating. There are lots of summer fruits and vegetables available and I stuck to range-fed lean meats and wild-raised fish. So like eating an elephant, you take it off one pound at a time just like you put it on. Although, I'll admit, it is always easier to put it on than taking it off.

Actually, this article isn't about losing weight at all. It is about how you transform anything. The same recipe applies. You want to change your behavior, your children's behavior, a bad habit, the results of your personal performance, your department, your company, etc. You change any of these things the same way…one step at a time.

- ✓ Identify specifically what you want to change.

- ✓ Create a reasonable plan.

- ✓ Start making small changes.

- ✓ Monitor and track results.

- ✓ Celebrate success.

- ✓ Repeat!

I've been celebrating my weight-loss success by buying new clothes. Actually, I haven't had an option as size 14 clothes look pretty terrible on a size 8 body which eventually became a size 4 body.

So what is it that you specifically want to or need to change? What have you known for a while that needs attention that you just haven't or didn't know how to get started or haven't been willing to commit to? What is a reasonable plan you could put in place? Make it attainable – don't set yourself up for failure – take your time and make it successful. What small changes can you begin to make that will compound over time?

There is no better time than the present to get started and I'll bet if you really want to make this change happen, there is nothing standing in your way except yourself. You can't achieve your goal if you never start so take that first step – it makes the second one so much easier.

I would tell you "good luck", but it really isn't about luck. It is about awareness of the need to change, shifting your mind set or paradigm about your current condition, committing, planning, tracking progress and celebrating success!

So what transformation do you want to achieve? How could you take the first step? How will you measure your progress? How will you celebrate your success? Plan the celebration now because you can do it. You can if you think you can and you can't if you think you can't.

My Story

My weight story continues. It has now been over two years since I lost those 55 pounds. And it is important to let you know that I have not found them again. I am delighted to tell you I've truly lost them. But just like the initial transformation or any transformation, keeping this weight off required I follow the same regimen. I know what I want (staying thin and healthy), I have a plan for doing it (veggies, fruits, lean open-range meats or wild-caught fish, and daily exercise), I measure (weigh frequently and monitor how clothes fit), and I celebrate. Sure, I have some chocolate once in a while or some wine or a beer once in a while. What would life be without chocolate?! I know this is a life's regimen for me, but I also know it is worth it. I love the transformative results and find the lifestyle required to be just another way of leading by example for my granddaughter, my family and anyone else that is observing. May all your transformations also be filled with rewarding results and life-long regimens you enjoy.

What is Employee Disengagement Costing Your Organization?

First of all, thank you to Chad Cook, President of Bright Side, Inc. Chad is a friend and colleague from Ohio who provided the impetus for this message. He shared with me an article, "The High Cost of Employee Disengagement", which I felt was not only informative, but also quite startling. (http://www.wistechnology.com/articles/983) As a leader of your organization you are also likely to find the content disturbing because it presents a tremendous challenge for leaders everywhere. I suspect we all think we are doing a better job than we really are.

I am in the midst of an organizational assessment for a regional professional service firm. Fortunately, I am finding the vast majority of their employees are engaged which is demonstrated through their hard work and committed to results. Further, the great news is the leaders want to know how the entire organization can be more successful, thus the request to conduct the assessment. While most of their employees are already engaged, I want to help them see the ROI potential they have by providing the direction and culture through which ALL the employees can and want to be fully engaged.

The Gallup Organization's most recent Employee Engagement Index reports:

- Active disengagement costs the US $300 billion a year in lost productivity at a time when we cannot afford it. So just imagine the positive impact on our economy if we could turn this around.

- 17% or 22.5 million workers are actively disengaged (unhappy, busy acting out their frustrations, angry, alienated, poisoning others, involved in idle chatter, etc.).

- Each one of these disengaged employees costs their employer $13K per year in lost productivity.

- Only 22% of workers are truly engaged working with passion and commitment to their company.

- At least 71% are on cruise control.

So why do 7 out of 10 workers feel a high degree of apathy? And, more importantly, what can you as a leader do to avoid this drain on your organization?

For decades, employees have been saying the same thing in almost every employee survey report. The vast majority of employee lack of engagement is because of these concerns:

- Managers whom they perceive do not care about them.

- Lack of clarity about the goals of their organization.

- Poor communications and the lack of information needed to do their job well.

- Information about company and their own performance not being shared.

- Their perceived inability to influence the results of the organization.

- Weak accountability.

- Having to work harder, longer hours while doing more with less.

Those of us in the organizational development (OD) profession would say the disengagement comes from a lack of an effective organizational culture. A culture that lacks leadership, a clear vision of where the organization is going, an appropriate organizational structure, accountability and measurements of success, an intentional communications systems. When employees have clarity about where the organization is going and how they can add value, when they believe their manager cares about their welfare and their contribution, they feel respected, valued and are rewarded appropriately; and when they have the information and tools to do their job well, the vast majority of the time they will be engaged, committed and contribute positively. This is true even in the midst of having to do more with less as those highly effective leaders are empathetic and realize in tough times effective communication and leading by example are even more important. These are imperatives for a successful organization.

So if you have an abundance of "water cooler conversations" going on in your own organization, take a quick assessment of what might be missing from your culture that is allowing so many employees to spend some portion of their time unproductively. Leading by example and holding everyone accountable for results are critical to producing results through highly satisfied employees. All our organizations lose some portion of revenue to non-productive disengagement. How badly is your revenue stream being impacted by this factor? What is it worth to you to turn this around? Would you like additional revenue without having additional labor expense?

My Story

I remember vividly experiencing first-hand employee disengagement. Downsizing or rightsizing or reduction in force or whatever it happened to be called at the time always made we wonder if I was next. And while I didn't knowingly want to contribute to the high cost of this disengagement, I'm sure I did my share of rationalizing with others and participating in the water cooler conversations. I tried to steer clear of the mainstream of this activity, but I know I did some of it. It is hard not too when you are significantly effected both emotionally and often financially.

On one occasion I particularly remember fearing that I would be a victim of a cost-cutting program. I was within days of being vested for retirement benefits which not only meant receiving a pension, but also health care benefits as a retiree. I thought for sure those who were in this situation would be laid off because not only would we help the company save money now, not having us on the payroll would also help them save money in future years.

Several years later I had the grueling task of helping determine staff-reduction decision-making criteria. In hind sight I know these decisions were made as fairly as possible based upon factual criteria such as current and past job performance, ability to contribute to future success of the company, and significance of current job responsibilities. Longevity with the company (i.e., being retirement eligible) was one of the last considerations and seldom had any bearing at all on reduction decisions. However, emotional rather than rational thinking often dominates when you are in the midst of stressful situations.

I knew my best bet for not being one of the reduction-in-staff candidates was to 1) manage my attitude 2) contribute to my organizations success through exceptional job performance 3) help others on my team be successful and 4) avoid being involved in employee-disengagement activities. While these criteria won't guarantee total job security, they are certainly helpful in reducing the stress you feel during these trying events. You at least have the assurance that you've done all you can to add value and this is what most employers expect.

Yes, You Can!

Fall brings renewal in many forms. School is about to start, marching bands are practicing, the Ryder Cup team is about to be announced, football teams are practicing and everyone one of them is predicting they will be the Super Bowl winner. If you follow football you are delighted when this time of year rolls around. Whether you are a football fan or not, I'm hoping this topic will be of interest to you. I'll admit I don't follow football much any more, but in the Orange Crush days, I was a big Denver Bronco fan. Recently, Floyd Little, # 44 for the Denver Broncos, was inducted into the Pro Football Hall of Fame. He had some mighty inspiring words in his acceptance speech which prompted this article.

Floyd graduated from the School of Hard Knocks into the Hall of Fame. This is not a new story for many Hall of Famers, but what is unique about Floyd's journey is he is still inspiring and encouraging young people because of it. He was kicked out of school, told by his teachers he couldn't learn, told by his coaches he couldn't play, was even fired by Coach Lou Saban from the Bronco squad in 1968 for fumbling the ball during a Buffalo Bills game, and had every opportunity to make negative choices along the way. He was angry and his father wasn't around. His father did continue to speak to him though even though he was deceased.

Floyd kept hearing his father say, "I've chosen you to do what I couldn't do". Those words helped Floyd realize he had a choice – he could remain angry and listen to the many belittling messages around him, or he could use his strength to a better advantage. Patience, persistence and passion were Floyd's guidelines along the way. He believed he could and he did. So can you.

While each of our stories and journeys are unique, we each encounter situations along the way where we have choices. We can all choose to listen to the naysayers, those who would have us believe we can't when we do have the option to believe we can.

I believe this is an important message particularly at this time in our country. We need and our youth need all the positive messages they can get. They need demonstrated evidence that what they believe in can and will become a reality.

While listening to the XM radio broadcast of the PGA Championship from Whistling Strait, one of the interviews was of Al Geiberger who was the first professional golfer to score 59. He commented that he believes it is more important to teach others how to do something than for him to have the great score him self. What a leadership statement! Wanting to help others achieve rather than focusing on his own personal achievement is certainly a rarity in business today and a demonstration of selfless leadership.

Well, I can tell you I get excited when I am in the low 90's let alone hitting a 59. But his point is well taken. Our personal success is often magnified and made more meaningful many times over when it is achieved through others rather than for ourselves.

I had the thrill this week of introducing my 7-year old granddaughter, Keara, to the game my husband and I love so much. She took her first two golf lessons and then my husband and I played 9 holes with her. She did a great job of listening, trying, and seeing results. What a great way to instill in her a belief that she can be successful and see the results of her hard work. The pride, fun and joy of teaching her is so much more rewarding than the struggle I go through to get a low score my self.

So I ask you, will you be able to say at the end of your next task…your current position…your career…the same words Floyd Little spoke at the end of his acceptance speech, "I've given you the best I've got, and I'm a better person for it"? Despite what life sends our way, we can, and most of us will.

My Story

My personal mission for many years has been to build skill and capability in others. I try to make my personal optimism and positive beliefs a model and through my professional skills help others improve their own personal and/or organizational skill and capability. *Where Passion Meets Performance* is my belief and company motto.

I got this "can do" attitude from my father. I remember when I was learning to drive a car he took me out to drive one Sunday afternoon. We stopped at the gas station to get some gas. He put the gas in the car and then said go ahead and drive around the block a few times. I'll be right here waiting for you. I was nervous and a bit flabbergasted to "go it alone". I made it around the block a few times without running into anything. I didn't think of it consciously at the time, but this was just one more way my Dad was saying, "I have confidence in you. You can do it. Just go make it happen." Thanks Dad for helping me know I can even when I think I can't.

You Are Never Too Old!

How many times have you thought, "If I had just ……." Hindsight is just so much more insightful than foresight it seems. When it comes to what we "coulda, shoulda, woulda", the good news is it is never too late to become what you want to be and we're never to old to reinvent ourselves.

Just think of all the times you've heard inspiring stories of older people going back to school completing college degrees with kids younger than their grandchildren. Recognizing that we can become something different or we can transform our businesses or we can achieve what we dream of…is particularly appropriate in these times of economic challenge.

I'm reminded of Betty White, the energetic much-older actress who continually gets new roles because she lives by this belief. When asked, "When are you going to retire?" Her response was, "When I'm no longer asked for." As long as we're being asked for, we still have a passion for using our talents and striving to move forward…it's never too late.

I want to thank my friend, Susan Brooks (http://www.servesyouright.net) for prompting this reminder. I just finished reading her wonderfully positive book entitled, *Serves You Right!*, which is packed full of stories about how faux pas turned into successes, bloopers became bonuses and blushes of embarrassment were overcome by smiles. While her messages focus primarily on customer service, I believe the same mantra is true of life in general. What better time to echo this reminder than when so many feel so down and out.

I currently have clients who:

- Have lost their business and are retooling themselves into new entrepreneurs.

- Have such slim margins they worry every day they might lose their business.

- Are in financial difficulty because of promises others made, but didn't keep, legal concerns, or other misfortunes.

- Can't get business financing because of the constraints of banks…and on and on and on.

By the same token, I have clients who are thriving in a wide variety of enterprises despite the economy. It is inspiring to witness their belief that they aren't too old, too tired, too stressed, too discouraged to reinvent themselves and survive and even thrive. They are:

- Reinvigorating their passion by breathing new life into their business.

- Taking an honest appraisal of their options and finding new creative sources of revenue.

- Finding non-traditional sources of funding and being more conservative in their growth strategy.

- Creating an entirely new line of products which service a different market…and the list goes on.

In all cases they are being rigorous in their discipline to create and use faithfully their strategic plans to guide and grow their businesses.

As always, if we look for gloom and doom the skies will turn gray, and if we look for positive signs and possibilities we will find sunshine.

So what are you wishing you had done? What are you thinking you are too old to do? What are you enduring in your business or your life in general that could be different, more positive, a fulfilment of your dreams? What do you choose to do about it? Because, as the title says, you are never too old to become what you coulda, woulda, shoulda. Now is the time to assess, plan and make what you want or are dreaming of your reality!

My Story

I want to thank you all for continuing to contribute to Social Security. At least for the time being there is still sufficient money to fund it and I've accumulated enough years to be eligible. I always felt that while I was paying in all those years, I was thankful my parents and my husband's parents were able to use it. Now I thank you.

At this stage in my life I want to do new things, learn more, have different experiences. I'm not the least bit interested in saying I coulda, woulda, shoulda in a few years. I want to be able to say I could, I wanted to and I did. So in addition to focusing on my health and family, I'll add concentrating on learning a bit more French and some Italian, and I'll re-write a cookbook I wrote years ago. It was called *Delicious Therapy* because that is what cooking is to me. However, I know now I would not cook most of the things that are in it. This version will be more lean and more green so I'll continue to be healthy enough to avoid the coulda, woulda, shoulda syndrome.

CHAPTER 4
Solutions

Breaking Out of the Box

Do you find yourself stuck in the proverbial box? Can't figure out how to get out of it? Do you wish you were more creative, innovative, original?

I've often wished I were more intuitive and creative. I admire people who have intuition and creative ability. I marvel at their sense of originality. My sister is a very talented, fine artist and compared to her I have always felt I had very little creativity.

I don't have any empirical research to back up my hunch, but I'd bet that one of the reasons we often have difficulty getting "out of our box" is that we simply don't slow down long enough to listen to the intuition we do possess. I know it is very easy for me to get caught up in the activity trap and not spend enough time in simple reflection. Creativity often comes from listening to our intuition, but we can't listen if our minds are talking to us rather than letting our minds listen to our own voice.

Look what happens when we take the time to intentionally "get out of our box". Here are three examples of how I've been able to tap into my creative side and take a non-traditional approach to an age-old dilemma. The age-old dilemma is how to get the business of a potential client or even get in the door. My "out of the box" approach follows....and by the way, I got the business.

- ✓ I wanted to meet an influential person who was on a Board of Directors so I offered to design and facilitate the Board of Directors retreats on a pro bono basis.
  Out of the Box Thinking - Find a creative way to meet those who make the decisions!

- ✓ I wanted to be the provider of choice for selected topics for programs offered through a community college so I made it a point to meet each of the members of the College Board of Directors.
  Out of the Box Thinking - Figure out who has the power to influence the decisions!

- ✓ By inquiring about the typical work pattern at a potential client site, I figured out when the key Director I wanted to meet would most likely be in the office. By dropping in at an opportune time, I was able to get an impromptu meeting with the Director I needed to see.
  Out of the Box Thinking – Find out when the person you need to meet is most probably available.

I know if I stop and listen to my intuition, if I intentionally get out of my "activity-trap box", I am just as creative as my fine-arts sister, but in a very different way. While she can take ordinary things and make them beautiful, I can take ordinary situations and turn them into business results. Creativity comes in all shapes and sizes. Don't box yourself in by thinking creativity is the sole possession of artists. Try it, I'll bet you can do it too!

My Story

I remember back in the mid-80s hearing the mantra being admonished that we should work smarter not harder. I know my superiors wanted us to improve processes, innovate, get out of our boxes and think differently, but I simply didn't know what they meant by working smarter not harder. After all, I wasn't intentionally doing stupid things and I was working as smartly as I knew how to do. Did they mean I was somehow supposed to be able to actually increase my intelligence? It seemed that way to me.

I now realize that leaders have to do more than provide the mantra. They have to help people understand what the mantra means and how to do it. I needed some examples, I needed demonstrations, I needed guidance. As Yogi Bear would say, "I'm as smart as the average bear", and I know I wasn't the only one that felt bewildered about what I should be doing differently.

I know as the article above says, I was probably caught up in the activity trap and if I had just slowed down a bit, I would have realized my superiors were simply asking me to use my intelligence in more innovative, creative, wise ways, not actually suggesting I get smarter which is how it seemed to come across to me. I hope as I matured, I became a wiser leader myself and provided more than just a mantra but rather became the example I wanted others to be.

Build It...They Will Come and Stay!

Like most American businesses you probably would like a quick fix, an easy elixir, a sure-fired solution to employee turnover, finding the best AND keeping them, creating a rewarding and resilient place to work, and along the way making some profit. It is easy to hope for solutions, but hope isn't a strategy. So how do those organizations that get named to one of the "best places to work" lists do it?

I have not made a study of the companies that have been named to these lists, but I can pretty safely bet that at the core they all share some common components. Of course, these components will look a bit different, take on a different flavor, play out differently from company to company, but at the heart of all of them I suspect they share a few common ingredients. Among these are:

Core Values – They each know the principles and values upon which they are building a solid foundation. They know and talk about what they expect from their leadership and their employees. Underpinning the behaviors of such companies are the principles of respect, trust, service-delivery, community citizenship, and recognition and reward.

Goals – Goals are defined, shared and results tracked. Everyone knows what they are striving for, how it will help the company and themselves. Results are monitored, rewarded and reinforced universally.

Human Capital – Human capital is managed as seriously as the organization's financial capital. Finding, employing and keeping the right talent and fitting each person for the necessary roles within the company impacts their ability to service clients and realize a profit. One client I had a few years ago had 100% turnover...and wondered how they could become more profitable! The revolving door of employees seriously erodes corporate culture and performance. Dissatisfaction breeds unhappiness so managing human capital with intent and skill is the keystone to corporate profits. As you can imagine, it was pretty easy to help this client improve their profits by getting control of their recruiting, hiring, training and recognition and reward processes.

Communication and Listening – People listen and share information with the intent to understand and gain understanding before offering a rebuttal. Teamwork, collaboration, trust, respect and workplace satisfaction cannot be optimized without focused and intentionally-managed effective communications.

Community – Everyone has a sense of community, of caring and of being cared for. A sense of community in the workplace goes way back to the Hawthorne studies in 1933. The more we believe people care about us and care for us the more we reciprocate and contribute. Profits, robust culture and wanting to be at work all suffer if a sense of community is absent in the workplace. It's the common bond that binds and allows profitability to grow.

Leadership – Leading by example is the simplest way to explain what people expect. If leaders themselves exemplify what they expect of their followers, leadership is much easier. You don't learn to be a leader by following some B-school set of books or formulas. You learn to lead by simply living the example of what you expect of your employees and what you see demonstrated by leaders you admire.

If you have built it and they are coming, but not staying you might examine this short list above to identify what's missing. Why are people leaving? While sometimes people leave for more money, often it is because they don't find the sense of community, engagement, and enrichment they need in order to grow, thrive and contribute fully.

The intent of every business owner is to build a successful organization, and of course, they want low turnover and few personnel issues because dealing with the soft stuff is always the hard stuff. I know the ingredients I've listed are core to being the best, but what is so rewarding is to see it play out before your very eyes in a company you know first hand.

My Story

My understanding of the key ingredients I prescribe above came to me in the late 70's when I first read the work of John D. Adams, Ph.D., who has spent his life studying and writing about work-life balance and the sense of community people seek in their lives. His writing is what first exposed me to the importance of core values and the need for a sense of community in the work place.

At this point I have to stop and brag a second. What caused me to write on this particular topic was something that happened to my son's company. Actually, it is a company co-founded by my husband and son and a good friend of my son's. Peaksware, LLC (www.trainingpeaks.com) was named as one of America's Best Places to Work by *Outside Magazine*. Peaksware exemplifies all the qualities I've written about above. Because of the core beliefs of the owners and a lot of hard work to live their values, they are not only attracting the best, the employees are choosing to stay.

I know the founders of Peaksware are not aware of Adams' work, yet because of their own personal values and beliefs they have created the environment he said was necessary to create employee happiness, an enriching work place and an environment that promotes both personal and business growth.

Thank you for letting me brag just a bit.

Building Excellence in Teams

Effective performance is a goal of every organization. And for most organizations this translates into having effective team performance because our activities and, therefore our results, are so interdependent. Achieving effective performance doesn't just happen. It requires intentional development, diligent work, and perseverance. It is helpful to have a guide. What are the important component parts? What are the necessary key factors? Is one order of developing the key components of a team better than another?

Excellence in organizational culture is a development process that enhances the effectiveness of work, impacts the results of individuals and groups, and provides the structure for successful and truly engaging, energizing environments.

Below I have provided a model for building effective performance. These are certainly not all the factors involved because people are people and, therefore, unpredictable. However, I am certain if a group of people who are to achieve business success lack many of these key elements, the probability of their success will be significantly diminished.

Team Excellence Model

Team Definition
*Charter, Mission and Goals

*Team Roles and Expectations

*Deliverables, Milestones and Timeline

Team Climate
*Trustworthiness

*Candor and Collaboration

*Focus on Excellence

Effective

Performance

Cycle

How We Work
*Norms and Operating Agreements

*Boundaries

*Stages of Growth

*Linkage - Communication within and Among Groups

Skills Used/Needed
*Competency and Technical Skill of Team Members

*Decision-making and Analytical Tools

*Process Improvement and Problem Solving Tools

Develop a team by addressing the key elements in a clockwise manner. Clarity of purpose and definition are fundamental followed by learning to work effectively as a unit. The skills the members possess can not be used optimally if the group does not know how to work well together so application of skills for the group's benefit follows effectively working together. Team

Climate is last because it is the composite of all the other factors. When the team has a good foundation, knows how to work well together and applies their collective skills, they have the opportunity to build a rich, positive, productive climate.

Team Definition

A group of people who are to achieve a designated business task need to have clarity about their goals, outcomes and expectations. It is helpful to set forth a charter which explains the mission and goals of the group along with the roles to be played by the members, expectations of the individuals and of the team as a whole, defined deliverables, milestones and a timeline for achieving their goals. The more clarity the group has the higher the probability they will be successful. So set up the group for success by providing as much clarity as possible at the outset.

How We Work

Teams don't gel without first going through some initial formation. It helps a team coalesce more quickly if norms and operating agreements are formed by the team up front. Help them get clarity about their boundaries of authority and responsibility as well as defining their reporting mechanisms and responsibilities for documentation. The more the members understand their relationships and dependency upon other groups and on each other, the quicker they will move through (and moving through not getting stuck is the operative word) the primary stages of team formation – Form, Storm, Norm and Perform.

First teams form which includes clarifying goals, understanding their roles and figuring how to work together. Then there is a bit of storming as they sort out responsibilities, makes attempts at solving problems and working through issues. Stage three is when teams develop their norms of operation, leadership emerges and individual contributions begin to surface. Performing is the stage where results really begin to occur and group processes become more refined. All teams go through all four stages, but they will move through them more quickly if they have good leadership and clarity about their purpose and functional expectations in the beginning.

Skills Used/Needed

Just because individuals are highly competent and skilled in their own right doesn't mean the group will function effectively as a team. Individual players don't always make good team players so it is important to provide training to help the individuals learn to be skilled team members.

You've probably heard the old adage there is no "I" in TEAM. I've seen many teams struggle because they were composed of highly skilled, very proud individuals who simply didn't know how to help the team as a whole be successful rather than focusing on their own individual successes. It is extremely important to clear the air of individual egos by providing tools and methods for group decision-making, and providing a set of standardized problem-solving techniques.

One of the most important, yet often overlooked tools is a way for team members to know themselves and their team mates more thoroughly. Simple profiles such as DISC* or Myers-Briggs are easy to understand, inexpensive and invaluable for gaining personal insight as well as understanding the group dynamics of the team. How can you expect a group to function effectively if you don't first help them know their own team composition and the often hidden dynamics that can either cause failure or set them up for success?

* DISC and the various aspects of this behavioral profile are the registered trademarks of Target Training International, Ltd.

Team Climate

We've all experienced times when we have been in a group that just felt right, it clicked, it just seemed to sail along smoothly without any ripples or snags along the way. What made this group work so well for you? Why did it seem so easy to get things done? I'll bet it was in large part because there was a team climate that allowed everyone to do their best without strife getting in the way.

Some of the elements of an effective team climate are establishing a climate of candor, honesty and respectfulness which allows everyone to feel trusted and know that others will behave in a trustworthy manner. Defining success and tracking progress through objective measurement helps everyone see how their part is contributing to success and that others are pulling their weight.

Measurement and objective feedback provide an equitable basis for consequences for everyone in the group, both positive and negative. Everyone knows where they stand and what their efforts are producing. Celebrations are based upon results and everyone knows what they did to help achieve the results that were produced. We all do what we do because of what happens to us when we do it so the more we get feedback and celebrate results (or take corrective action where and when needed), the more positive results the group will achieve.

Which parts of the Team Excellence Model are working well for your group? Where do you need to focus your energy to help the group be more successful? Do you have well-defined charters and expectations for the groups in your organization? Is there an esprit de corps which allows for candor, honesty and trustworthy communication within and among the teams? Above all, are you functioning as a trustworthy leader yourself? If so, you are well on your way to building team excellence within your organization.

My Story

As in most situations, I developed this model because of a need. I was fortunate to get a retainer contract very soon after starting my consulting practice. The company didn't have an organizational development staff, but they knew they had needs. They did have a skilled Human Resource department so my role was to develop and implement processes that the HR department could then administer. They were in the midst of launching teams when I took the contract so it was critical to create an easy-to-understand model that could serve for any and all teams in the organization.

No matter the size of the team or the level of the team's responsibility, this model works. First members have to understand their mission and then understand how to work effectively together in order to optimally apply their individual and collective skills. And lastly, in order to optimize their effectiveness and create an environment where all members can thrive, a team climate must exist that is enriching, engaging, and empowering.

Communication During Times of Crisis

I have recently aided several clients with policy development for their organizations. This work made it clear that no matter what the crisis, when there is a major disaster leadership, and communications are vital. Let's explore the importance of good communications before, during and after a major crisis.

Oh, My Gosh! No Phones!

You probably have a list of emergency phone numbers and contacts in your contingency plans. But what if both land lines and cell phones don't work? Do you have a method in your contingency plan that tells people where to get information when it is impossible to reach them. For example, is there a centralized community bulletin board or community emergency disaster center for your area? Or consider establishing an emergency internet site which even in a time of non-emergency tells people what to do in case something occurs. Think this can't happen to you? Think again because this happens every year due to fires, tornados, flood and other traumatic situations.

Remote Contacts and Storage Locations

That emergency contact list you have for all employees, does it list people who live with them or contacts in another area? Consider asking for a contact that doesn't live in the area in case the entire area is affected by a disaster.

Double check to ensure all of your information is stored in a safe place – not near where you are. It is likely that you have an emergency contact list off site – possibly at your home or at your HR manager's home. Sounds safe, but in the case of floods, large fires, or tornados many homes and businesses in a large area are destroyed. Think about storing a copy in a remote location or use a commercial vendor to store confidential data. A friend of mine is an HR VP for a company that was in the World Trade Center. Fortunately, she had a copy of all their employee contacts in another state so she could readily get access to vital information.

Top of Mind Questions

The most important questions after finding out if family members are safe are all about leadership. Things like…

Do I still have a job? Will my benefits continue?   Where will I find temporary housing and what about school and day care? How will I get paid if I am not in the immediate area? How will my insurance claims be handled if I have to use out-of-network providers? Can the Employee Assistance Program help me and how can I reach them? And on and on.

How Can I Help?

Also anticipate the communication needs of employees who are not affected. They want to help, but need to know how to do so and what help is needed. Again the community disaster bulletin board or an emergency internet site can be very helpful. Leaders need to be prepared to address the survivors who often have unaffected guilt feelings as well as the emotions and needs of those directly impacted.

Of course, my hope is that no one ever has to deal with these concerns, but as the leaders of our organizations we have the obligation to be prepared.

My Story

At a former employer, I helped the Human Resource Department lead the effort to create disaster recovery practices and policies throughout the organization. We were located far enough away from other emergency services that we had to do all we could to be self-supported.

I was reminded again how important this was during the terrible minutes following the 9/11 attacks. A colleague and postgraduate friend of mine was the Human Resource Manager for Lehman Brothers whose offices were in the World Trade Center Towers. She was en route to work via the New Jersey/Manhattan ferry when the first attack occurred so she immediately turned around and took the next ferry back to New Jersey. Her first action after calling her husband was to call all the senior leaders of the firm. The management team gathered on the New Jersey shore and immediately started using their phone tree. You see, they had done their disaster preparedness homework which included an offsite list of all employees and their emergency contact information. Within hours of the disaster occurring, they were able to locate all the Lehman employees and all were safely out of the building. So in the midst of a national disaster there was a reason to have hope for others. Just think of how daunting the task of finding and contacting all the employees would have been without this emergency preparedness forethought.

Communications Matrix

Sometimes we make difficult things more difficult than they need to be. The need for better communication within organizations is a topic that is top of mind for every leader with whom I've ever worked. Leaders certainly agree that effective communication is one of their biggest challenges. Even when they believe they are doing everything they know how to do to keep others well-informed and work very hard at communicating well, employees invariable say the organization needs to improve communications.

I always feel when a leader asks me to help them improve communication that I've been asked to solve world hunger. It is a huge topic, everyone seems to have a different opinion of what is needed, and it is impossible to satisfy everyone.

Hopefully the matrix below will help you determine the type of method and frequency needed to ensure communications are conveyed in an effective manner and for the appropriate audience in your organization.

Communications Matrix

A Decision Matrix for Guiding Effective Communication

	Low	High
High	One-on-One Dialog	One-on-One Dialog
E	Written and Oral	Written and Oral
M	Present Multiple Times	Present Multiple Times
O		Consider Including Audio Visual Aids
T		
I	Mass Delivery is Acceptable	Group Delivery Initially Followed by
O	Written or Oral	One-on-One Opportunity for Questions
N	Minimal Questions Will Arise	Provide Written Material for Complex Topics
Low		

Complexity of Topic from Receiver's Perspective

High Emotion and High Complexity

Topics with high emotional content and high complexity require individual conversations, both oral and written explanations and need to be presented multiple times. The higher the emotional content the less the recipient is likely to actually hear what you are saying. They will hear the words, but as soon as their emotion takes over, the message gets lost. Therefore, it is critical the message be presented over and over and over. If you think you've said it enough, say it again. Also provide the message both orally and in written form so the recipient can study the content and facts. Video presentations or DVD are also effective if the topic impacts the recipient's family so they can watch it together and have a discussion in the privacy of their home. Allow plenty of time for questions and dialog to sort through the complex facts and the complex emotions. An example of this topic is a change in 401(k) options or changes in other complex benefits offerings or any changes to pay and compensation. What are examples of this type of communication in your organization? How have you delivered this type of message in the past? How might you change your approach in the future?

Low Emotion and High Complexity

Low emotional topics, but that are of a complex nature can be initially delivered as a group because the content won't evoke emotions. However, the topic needs to be reviewed multiple times and written materials also need to be provided because the subject is complex. Allow sufficient time to answer questions and help people understand the subject. An example of this topic is a change to a work procedure that has many steps or a new method of work processing. How are you conveying this type of information currently? Do you need to adjust your approach in the future?

High Emotion and Low Complexity

Because of the low complexity the content can be presented orally. There is no need for written materials because the subject will be easily understood. However, because there is high emotion you need to provide sufficient time to ask questions, provide dialog and process any emotional outpouring that might occur. A change in work schedules is an example of this category. It is not complex because all those involved understand the work day and general hours of work. However, there can be a lot of emotional content involved in changing people's work hours because it disrupts their routine, that of their family, their transportation pattern, possibly their co-workers will be in a different group, and a myriad of other seemingly ordinary, but nonetheless, emotional changes. Don't under estimate how complex, seemingly low-complexity issues can be due to the emotional impact.

Low Emotion and Low Complexity

These topics are the easiest to communicate effectively because they are generally factual and don't cause emotional concern for the recipient. Messages such as these can be delivered in mass, via email, via voice mail, as stuffers in pay checks, on bulletin boards or via other mass methods. Be sure the common questions that will arise are answered as a part of the communication, but otherwise these messages can be handled in an efficient manner allowing for a minimum of questions. Topics such as building maintenance items and general office announcements fit this category.

If you stop to ask yourself two questions before launching communications you'll save yourself a lot of work and avoid a lot of confusion. These two questions are: 1) what is the emotional content of the message to the intended recipients and, 2) how complex is the topic to the recipients. Then select the method of conveying the message accordingly.

My Story

I want to thank Bob Berman, Executive Vice President for Human Resources of Eastman Kodak Company, for this matrix. I was one of the Division HR managers that reported to Bob. He was a great communicator and knew others needed help with this important topic. We focused a lot of attention on providing templates for managers to use to 1) improve their own skills and knowledge and 2) drive consistency throughout our divisions. One principle we lived by was to try to make these templates as simple and easy to use as possible. This matrix is one of the examples of these tools we created to aid consistent and appropriate communications. Thanks, Bob. This simple tool has continued to be very useful to me personally and I have shared it with many client organizations also. I hope it is helpful to you also.

Content versus Process – Your Role and Mine

You know the old adage..."there are two kinds of people in the world". There are many ways to look at this dichotomy – men and women, old and young, tall and short, and so on. I'd add another. There are process people and those who feel process gets in the way of the content. I'm the process type. This article focuses on the valuable role a skilled facilitator can play in helping you achieve better results faster.

What is a facilitator?

A facilitator is a process person. Their job is to manage the process of information exchange, decision-making, discussion guidance, and effective group dynamics in order to achieve the results you are targeting for your work session. In short, the facilitator's responsibility is to address the journey rather than the destination. You and the other participants concentrate on the content and destination while the facilitator concentrates on the process and journey.

Why would you want to use a facilitator?

That's easy! Using a facilitator allows you and other group members the freedom to concentrate on the quality of the content and decisions, to optimize your time, and to maximize group effectiveness. Gee! With all those benefits, why wouldn't you want to use a facilitator?

Use a facilitator anytime you are concerned with...

➢ Both the decisions and how they are made...like when you are trying to move into a more participative style or when you are trying to embrace greater involvement.

➢ Optimizing the time invested by the group...like when you have a limited amount of time for the entire group to be together and you have to ensure an inclusive process and quality results.

➢ Reducing resistance and increasing buy-in...like when new decisions or changes are being introduced.

➢ Increasing communications and generating feedback or input toward problem resolution.

Accommodating and managing a variety of styles, interests, and agendas. In short, anytime you and your colleagues as content experts want to be free from managing the process, and need to optimize time, effort and results.

How do you specify your needs?

A good facilitator will know how to help you design the work session so you and your group achieve the results you desire, but it is helpful if you can...

➢ Articulate the outcomes you want to achieve.

➢ Characterize the perspectives of the participants.

➢ Share the norms the group currently uses.

➢ Lead by example so others are willing to give up their sense of control of the process in order to concentrate on the quality of the content and the decisions being made.

My Story

As a part of building organizational capability in a client company, I created a Facilitator's Training Program. The goal was to train a handful of employees in the skills and group dynamics necessary to facilitate employee meetings, team workshops, and customer-focus groups. So, of course, it was important early on to define facilitation, clarify the expectations of facilitators and differentiate the role that facilitators play versus the role of the group participants. The facilitator concentrates on the designs, orchestrates and focuses on the process so the participants can be fully engaged in effective decision-making.

Through a series of training sessions seven facilitators were developed and continue to service this client organization and often facilitate public meetings for gathering information from their clients and customers.

Getting Out of Your Stuckness

You know "stuckness". It's when you're at that point where you feel immobilized, confused, uncertain, stymied, numb, powerless, not in control and tired. It happens when you lose your job, lose a big contract, didn't get the promotion you expected, find out you have to move, get a divorce, are very ill, or some one you care about is very ill. You know, you've been there.

Know what? It also happens when good things that you look forward to happen. Like when get married (Oh, this is what it's like!), have a child (My gosh, will this kid ever sleep through the night?), get a promotion or a big new responsibility (Oh dear, can I do this?), or your child graduates (Yippee, but will they move back in?). Getting "stuck" happens both when sad and happy occasions occur.

Good News and Bad News

You don't think you've ever been there? Just wait!

Haven't been there in a while? Good!

You're there now? Welcome to the club – you are likely to find friends here.

Guess what? It will happen to you again (and again, and again).

Yep, that's right. It happens to all of us...multiple times. Some move through the physical, emotional, and psychological roller coaster of change quickly and for others it takes time. The key is to not get STUCK in the quagmire of change.

Warning Signs!

Fortunately, there are warning signs and if you heed them you'll become more resilient and get out of "stuckness" more quickly. Some of these signs are:

➢ A body part – you know which part it is. It will get sore, start to ache, act up.

➢ Breathing – holding your breathe or breathing too quickly – slow down, take deep breaths.

➢ Pace – faster than usual. You're rushing to get to some place you don't even want to go to.

➢ Sleeping pattern – either insomnia or wanting to sleep all the time; you are always tired.

When you see any of these warning signs, they are clear signals that you need to take stock, reflect, review your plan for getting life back in order and, if necessary, get help.

So what can I do to move on...get myself out of "stuckness" when it happens to me?

Here are a few tips...

✓ NORMAL and NECESSARY – stages of change happen to everyone – accept it as a fact.

✓ STEAM VALVES – find an outlet for frustration, anger, confusion.

✓ SUPPORT SYSTEM – accept the help and understanding of your friends and family.

✓ YOU – take care of yourself – maintain exercise, eat right, get rest.

✓ PLAN – reexamine, reflect and plan for how you can take steps to move forward – not giant steps, just take little steps continually and you'll find yourself climbing out of your despair.

My Story

People who have just lost their jobs can easily get stalled in the "stuckness stage". My first encounter with this specific title was a series of workshops I developed for Drake, Beam, Morin, Inc, a large outplacement service firm. As a part of their service, they offer a series of in-house seminars for clients whom they are helping to retool as they search for new employment. This just seemed like an accurate description of where many of these people were…stuckness. I know that isn't really a word, but you'd have difficulty convincing people in the midst of that quagmire of this fact because the feeling and the numbness are real.

I also worked with a large number of employees at Kodak who were also in this same position. The series of workshops there was called *The Challenge of Change*. One of the video's I found which I used as a teaching aid was by Dr. Ben Bissell, entitled *Managing Transition and Change*. He is the one I picked up the essence of this article from. It was great information presented in a humorous and engaging manner. People in these circumstances need some humor and Ben does a fabulous job of communicating a very serious topic in a funny, light-hearted way. Thanks, Ben, wherever you are these days.

Love the Life You Live and Live the Life You Love

The older I get the more powerful this saying is yet living this philosophy is challenging. If you saw the movie or play, *Chicago*, you may recall Renee Zellweger singing a similar line to Richard Gere from inside her jail cell. I certainly hope none of you ever face that set of circumstances, yet even in these circumstances she recognized she loved the life she lived despite the consequences of her choices. Can we each say the same about our lives?

One of my clients, Vickie McDermott, is a realtor to high-end clientele. I recently asked her if she was envious of the vast wealth many of her clients have. "No," she said. "My goal is to be happy in my life with balance in all aspects of it. I want to live with purpose and within my means." I had a great respect for her already, but my opinion was reinforced significantly by this statement. For her the grass isn't greener on the other side of the fence or stucco wall. She finds a way to see the green grass right where she is.

I have a few personal beliefs that help me stay centered and content:

✓ Know your personal mission – I know the purpose of my life and the value I am providing.

✓ Short-term goals with a future focus – If you have longer-term goals then near-term goals help you stay focused on those objectives while achieving results and accomplishments now. When I focus on my own plan and objectives I tend not to get caught up in unrealistic wishes or the lives of others.

✓ Be a realistic dreamer – Dreams are important. They cause us to stretch beyond where we are now while living in the reality of today.

✓ Know yourself well – Be self-aware, reflect and self-examine. This helps me stay focused on all the reasons to be content where I am rather than being envious of others.

✓ Surround yourself with positive people – We get what we focus on and those around us shape our world-view so choose to make it a positive picture. Doing so helps make our self-fulfilling prophecy positive and filled with possibilities.

What are your personal mantras that help keep you focused, balanced, and content with where you are in life? What cautions do you know you have to be wary of otherwise they overtake your sense of reality and contentedness?

My Story

Once in a while I see a movie that is go good, so entertaining, so insightful that I have to see it again. I watch it the first time for the story and just to see what it is about. Then I realize I need to see it again. The second time I take a note pad.

That was the case with the film, *Chicago* and *The Devil Wears Prada*. I reinforce learning (again) as I laugh or cry at the movie. The same is true with friends. I learn (again) and reinforce why these people are my friends as I reflect on our conversations.

Luck, Chance or Good Planning?

My sister believes I am the luckiest person she knows while my husband says there is no such thing as luck. He believes what sometimes appears to be luck is good preparation and diligently looking for opportunities. I'm sure you know people who seem to have a black cloud following them around and others who seem to be walking around with a rainbow and sunshine perpetually over their head. These people always seem to be at the right place at the right time. This is how my sister sees me. Personally, I side with my husband. What do you think is the winning combination?

I have always been a planner and goal setter. As I look back over my childhood I see all sorts of ways my parents were shaping me into the planner I became. My Dad, in particular, was always very optimistic and I followed in his footsteps. So this is likely why my sister thinks I am lucky. I also seem to have a natural knack for being able to see long-term and easily put together near-term goals that cumulatively lead me toward bigger goals. I don't get at all frustrated by continually chipping away at what seems to be far off.

In these tough economic times I believe having an attitude and belief that luck, good fortune or whatever you prefer to call it will come your way does, in fact, help it come your way. It's the old self-fulfilling prophecy ideas: the Pygmalion Effect. Without this perspective you may be unable to see the luck right in front of you if you are not well-prepared and actively looking for opportunities. When you change your focus you do change your life.

So what are a few very easy things you can do to put into the universe what you are looking for in the way of opportunities so when luck comes your direction you are prepared. Here are a few tips to get you started:

Pinpoint – Be as concise and precise about what you want as possible.

Pen/Pencil – Write down what you are looking for and the specific actions you are going to take to help make your wish become a reality. Magic begins to happen by writing down your desires and both consciously and subconsciously focusing on what you want.

Partner – Find a partner or friend with whom you'd like to share your written list. Sharing and getting support from others boosts the magic and makes what you want become more alive and concrete.

Post - Keep what you've written posted in front of you in your office or a handy place you see frequently. Focus and presence help you continually work toward your goals and also help you stay attuned to seeing the opportunities that are around you.

Progress – Share your progress with those you've shared your goals with. They are your support system and really want to cheer you on as you make advances.

Praise - Praise yourself for your achievements; those you've shared your goals with will want to praise you also. Feeling good about your hard work makes you want to work harder.

You'll be pleasantly surprised how effortless working toward your goals begins to feel and amazed at the good fortune that comes your way. Let me know how lucky you become.

My Story

Aubrey Daniels, a warm-hearted and very wise clinical psychologist who is often referred to as the Father of Performance Management, was instrumental in helping me understand how to pinpoint targeted goals, realize the importance of measurement and feedback, and celebration along the way. Ever since I've been practicing the simple, easy-to-use methods he provided. Luck appears to play a big part in our results at times, but behind the scenes you'll always find preparedness and alertness to opportunity.

My daughter-in-law has a sign in her office that sums it up. It says "Luck is a matter of preparation meeting opportunity". I believe this is an Oprah quote, but whomever said it was absolutely right. You have to follow the principle above in order to be prepared, but then you have to be on the lookout for opportunity.

Making Wishes Come True Requires Balance

Every year toward holiday time you hear a refrain about making a wish for the treasures little ones want, good tidings for others, resolutions to make goals come true, etc. Certainly it never hurts to dream, in fact, it helps a lot. What we dream about and dwell on often comes true. So be sure your wishes are what you really want and then plan to make them become a reality.

Here are some very interesting and, to me, disturbing statistics. Think about these stats for a minute and see if they apply to you.

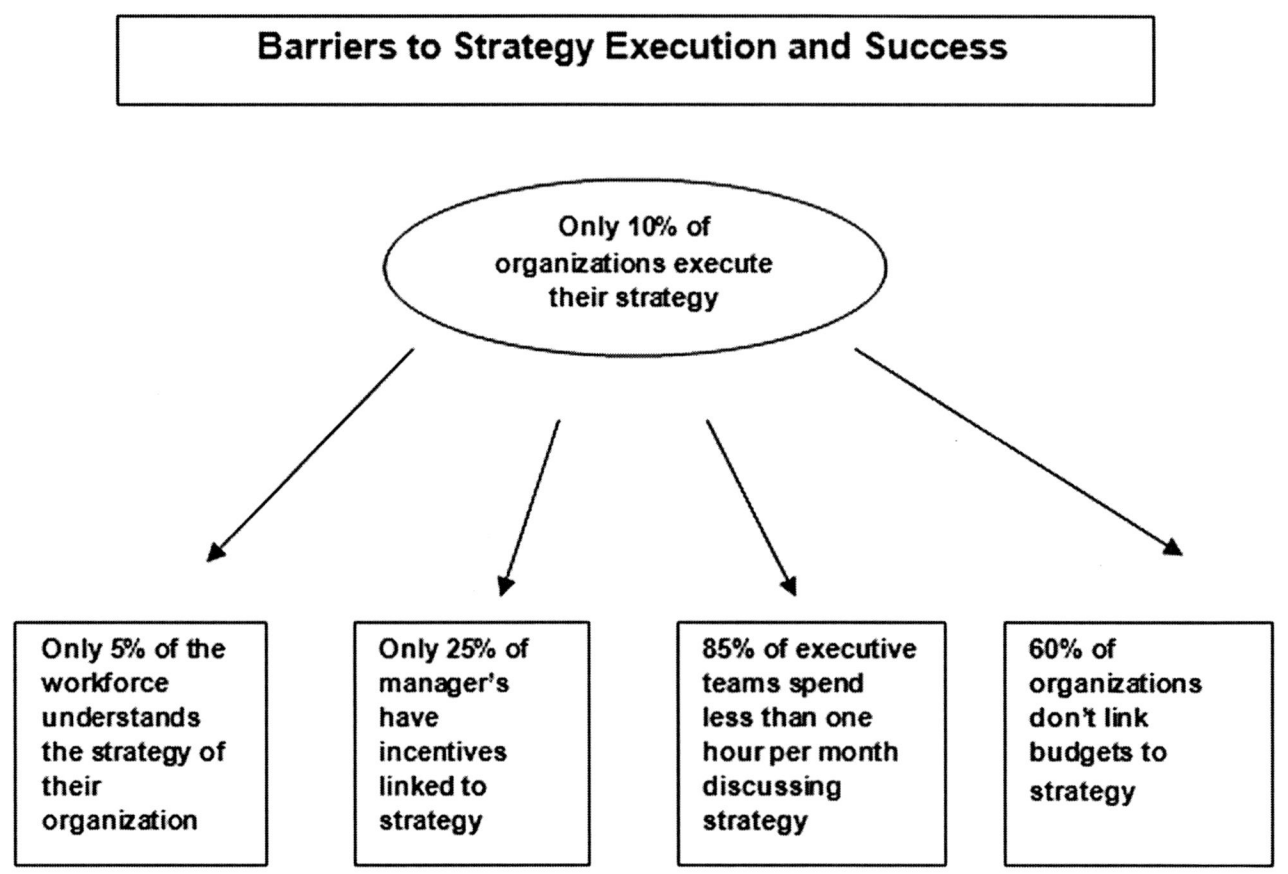

I find these data, which I found in a Harvard Business Review article, staggering. No wonder so many American workers have little commitment to their work. They don't know how they contribute so often their work lives have little meaning. A lot of research says people get involved as volunteers outside of work in order to find meaning and to contribute.

Could it be one reason for this is because so few find meaning at work? Add to this that only 25% of managers have their incentives linked to strategy, that executive teams discuss strategy and how to achieve goals less than one hour per month, and budgets aren't linked to how financial goals will be achieved. Is it any wonder why the best of the best make their wishes come true by not only having a strategy, but also by making sure there is alignment throughout the entire organization so that everyone understands where they are going, how they can contribute and what level of success has been achieved?

In a world where intangible assets are more and more valuable having a balanced strategy that includes not only financial goals, but also customer-focused, internal process and employee learning and growth goals is not only critical, but is one of the golden keys to building a vibrant, successful organization. A balanced approach to planning for and managing your business includes all 4 components: financials, customers, internal processes and employee learning and growth.

Here are a few more interesting facts. If you look at the physical assets of a company that are typically measured by traditional accounting methods, they compose less than one-fourth of the value of the corporation.

Fully three-quarters of the value of the average business today is in intangible assets (customer value, value-added services, intellectual capital, human capital, etc.). Yet most businesses spend the vast majority of their time only measuring and monitoring financial performance. The value of intangible assets in an organization continues to increase in value. The value of intangible assets has increased in importance by 37% over the past 30 years.

1982	1992	2006
38%	62%	75%

When the focus is only on achieving short-term financial targets, that's where everyone's attention is placed to the severe detriment of intangible assets which make up the majority of the organization's value.

Just think about your own business. What is the ratio of physical assets compared to the intellectual capital and knowledge of you and your employees, the internal processes you have developed to ensure quality customer products and services, the key employees you zealously protect. If all you had were the physical items in your business, what would you really have? You could see and hold a lot of things, but you wouldn't be able to see, service or deliver any of them without the intangible assets that bring value to those physical items.

I am making such a strong point of this because as the data above demonstrates only 10% of the organizations execute on their strategy. If this is true then even fewer organizations actually have a strategy. I know you want your wishes to come true, but how can they when most organizations spend so little time preparing, planning and executing their strategy?

To conclude on a more positive note, wishes really do come true through having a balanced approach to developing your strategy and then executing to your plan. In research done by the Hackett Group in 2002, it was discovered that 60% of Fortune 1000 companies have a Balanced Scorecard Strategy (Kaplan and Norton, Harvard) and use it to run their business and 96% of the largest global companies also use the same approach.

Lest you think using a Balanced Scorecard Strategy is "just for the big boys", think again. No matter the size of the organization, we all face exactly the same types of challenges – growing our businesses, ROI on our marketing and advertising efforts, improving employee retention, knowing what the competition is planning, controlling internal costs, reacting to regulations and their affect on our costs, and on and on and on.

So what is the value of the intangible assets in your company? Are your intangible assets just as valuable or maybe more valuable than your tangible assets? How are you investing in keeping your intangible assets current? How much time do you and your leadership team spend planning for and talking about your strategy? How are you tying recognition and reward to performance and results?

My Story

US companies are good at tracking financial results and this is likely true of companies worldwide. Unfortunately, we aren't nearly as diligent about stating, monitoring and tracking results in the areas that produce the financial results.

Does anyone really print money? Well, yes, I guess some people do, but I mean as a legal business enterprise can you really print and sell money? Banks make interest on loans, but even they can't actually print what they sell. So the only way we can really control our financial results is by managing effectively and prudently our stakeholder interactions, our internal processes and products, and management of our human assets.

I'll admit I was uninformed about the statistics above until I became aware of the tremendous impact of balanced business planning. Oh my gosh, what power and potential it provides.

Management in Toyland

Can you imagine what a catastrophe it would be if Santa didn't manage his workshop well? The elves would be running amuck and children everywhere would lose faith in the spirit, joy and hope of the Big Guy in Red. I can just picture it now...

✓ Instead of following the instructions and holding themselves accountable the elves didn't follow the "some assembly required" instructions so toys wouldn't work when they were delivered on Christmas morning.

✓ They had a list, but they weren't checking it twice so quality control was non-existent.

✓ Teamwork was being eroded by lots of petty bickering and talk behind the elves backs – just picture all those whispers about Rudolf's nose!

✓ Being good and nice got replaced with being bad and naughty; there were outbursts of crying and whining in the workshop – the HR department in Toyland was on overload.

✓ The sleigh and big bags for toys were waiting, but the elves hadn't followed the production plan so last-minute crisis and pandemonium reigned right up to the deadline on the 24th.

✓ The financial statement for Toyland is in the **RED** – there is so much waste, inefficiency and self-interest that Santa is about to declare bankruptcy!

What a dire picture, indeed! So to make Toyland run smoothly Santa's New Year's Resolution is for everyone...

✓ To know the mission, rules and procedures.

✓ To be treated with respect and dignity.

✓ To tell the truth...always.

✓ To make commitments and keep promises.

✓ To build in quality and do it right the first time.

✓ And for Santa to lead by example by taking a stand for what's right!

Sounds like a pretty good prescription for success whether you're the leader of Toyland or your own company, right?

My Story

You know those little freebie business magazines you sometimes get in the mail? I get them every once in a while and generally toss them into the round file. However, one came through that caught my eye. It was about how Santa Claus manages the North Pole. It happened to arrive around holiday time so I took a peak inside. It was the genesis of this article...just one more valuable gift from the Big Guy in the Red Suit.

Next In Line – Are You Ready?

Only Forty Percent Are Prepared

Often large, publicly held companies have formalized succession planning processes. Their fiduciary responsibility to their shareholders requires them to do so. However, private companies often overlook the need for this important activity even though their fiduciary responsibility to themselves, their families and their employees is no less than it is for larger corporations. If anything there is an even more heightened sense of emotional obligation, yet seldom is succession planning addressed in smaller organizations.

A recent study by Korn/Ferry International reported that only about 40% of organizations have adequate successors in place for their CEO position. Is the next person in line for an important position in your company ready? Do you have a process which ensures continuity and on-going success regardless of who is at the helm? Would your customers be happy if they knew you were relying on an ad hoc plan for ensuring service to them should something suddenly happen to you or one of your core leaders?

It is very easy to get caught up on the day-to-day operation of business and fail to focus on future preparation. After all, our own demise is not a topic we like to dwell on. It's tough to admit we are not indispensable.

One Size Doesn't Fit All

My husband and I both own small businesses. He and I both have to decide what we want to have happen to our business-es if and when we cannot or do not choose to continue actively running them. What's more, one solution is not the answer for every situation. What I choose to do and what the transition for my business should be is quite different than what my husband chooses for his businesses. Yet, together we have a common goal and obligation. Namely,

- Have a plan and share it with each other and other immediate family members.

- Well prepare those who might take over the business so they are ready to be successful and our clients don't suffer.

- Ensure personal finances and business finances can support the plan and do not experience any interruption.

- Ideally, plan well in advance so the transition for all parties involved can be smooth.

What fits your situation? Do you have adult children involved in the business who are interested in taking over leadership and have demonstrated technical and leadership capacity? If children are not involved or this option is inappropriate for your situation, do you have internal leaders who might be interested in succeeding you? How big is the gap between the current skills of those who might take over and the capacity and knowledge they need to have to be successor-ready? Do you need to consider a strategic external hire? Sometimes it is best to hire skill, talent and new blood in order to intentionally take the company to a new level, into a new market, or a new generation of products.

Will Your Company's Systems Help or Hurt the Transition

When we think of succession planning we naturally think of people. But one overlooked aspect of this important busi-ness activity is to also analyze your internal systems to be sure they support your transition plans. Do you have checks and balances set up or are your systems simply an evolution from the way you've always done business? Who has access to what type of information and who controls that access? Don't get caught in the trap of preparing the people only to find they are hamstrung by poorly designed internal policies, practices and procedures. Sure, they will be in a position to "fix it" if they are the new leader, but don't leave your undone work for them to fix when you want them concentrating on leading the business forward. It is as important to do an analysis of your systems to ensure they support effective growth and transition as it is to prepare the emerging leaders.

Managing the Transition

One of the biggest barriers to leadership succession is living under the illusion that we are in control. None of us are in control the way we like to think we are. Yet, giving up our sense of control and relinquishing responsibility to others is crucial. Grooming and mentoring others will fail if power isn't shared. Who are the best leaders you know? Who do you emulate and admire? I'll bet one of the reasons you admire them so much is because they are willing to share power and responsibility. So...

➢ Recognize the need for a Succession Plan for your organization.

➢ Develop a plan that is appropriate for the size, legal configuration and capacity needed for the on-going viability of your organization.

➢ Apply the plan you have developed to your particular situation, i.e., identify potential successors, decide how to develop any deficiencies they have, start coaching, mentoring and developing.

➢ Share the responsibility you have now so others gradually begin to accept it under your guidance.

➢ Reassess the plan and the development of others periodically to ensure what you are doing is working and still appropriate for your needs.

My Story

My first experience with succession planning involved managing the Gold Process for emerging leaders while working at for a large global corporation. This was a rigorous process of qualifying, grooming, coaching, mentoring and evaluating individuals with potential for higher management-level positions. This is one form of succession planning and it is important, but there are many other forms that are equally important and often overlooked.

My next encounter was for a client organization. My task was to create a process for managing the on-going viability of leadership throughout the organization. This is a very different view point than the Gold Process because it took a global approach. What did the data say about the longevity and age of current leaders in all positions? What processes had provided successful leaders in the past? Was it still a viable process for the future? Were there positions needed in the future that didn't even exist now? Was there a pool of available talent from which to hire or did they need to "grow their own" leaders? Could they create a process that fit the needs for all types of positions at every level in the organization? What were the skills and capabilities needed in the future and were they different than what had been needed in the past?

To shorten the story, yes, we did develop a universal process that worked for all positions and all levels. And it is still the model I use as a starting point anytime I set up a succession planning process. The key learning and difference in these two processes is to start by determining what kind of succession plan the company needs and then design the process accordingly. Many organizations focus on a few top positions because 1) they are viewed as critical positions, 2) they may be hard to fill, 3) they may require years of experience to gain the insight needed to be successful, 4) people in these positions carry a lot of responsibility so a lengthy void in these positions is harmful to the organization.

While these are all true statements, don't forget the rest of the employees are the ones who produce the products, have the institutional knowledge, service the customers and produce the revenue. They are equally important and may require a different type of succession planning process in order to avoid costly gaps in these positions.

Oh, no! It's Performance Review Time!

As if the general news wasn't enough to get you down, at least once a year the performance review process rears its ugly head in many companies. Having been a Human Resource division manager for several years, I can relate to this concern, but I also know it doesn't have to be this way. Why is it that so many people dread both writing and reviewing performance? As a leader, you have it in your power to make this periodic conversation one of recognition and encouragement or at least positive coaching and empowerment.

Here are a few reasons why Performance Reviews are dreaded by nearly everyone involved and some improvement suggestions:

- **Poor Training and Development** – Promotions often occur because of great individual contribution. Unfortunately they are often followed by little training and development on how to excel in the new position. If you are in this situation, ask your HR department or the leader you report to for training and coaching. Share with them your interest in continuing to be a star contributor, but to do so you need development for future growth.

- **Yes, But** – Often you are told how you've performed through the year and then the conversation quickly segues to a "yes, but" followed by what you need to do to improve. All the positive energy and good feeling you just created gets lost in the "yes, but" comments. Guess what the employee will remember? Avoid this problem by separating performance review and performance planning into two different conversations. Get the maximum value from the positive review euphoria. Then have a development planning conversation at a different time.

- **Poor Documentation Processes** – It is really difficult to remember accurately the specifics and details of a person's performance without good documentation throughout the year. Avoid this problem by keeping an active folder for each employee. This is simply a memory-jogger file for collecting specific performance notations that need to be included in the annual review. Once the official review documents have been completed, purge this file and start a new active file for the coming year. This is not an official performance file, but a place to keep your own notes so you more accurately provide details to the employee. One of a leaders major responsibilities is the effective development of people. So it behooves you to have an effective process for providing feedback and on-going development.

- **Generalities** – Not providing specific examples is a real downer for employees. Being told you did a good job but not being reminded of what you did and why your mangers believes you did such a good job or receiving coaching without specifics on what needs to be improved and how to do it provides nothing to grow on. Make sure you keep detailed notes in your active file mentioned above. Cite specific examples and solid reasons for your comments.

- **No Surprises** – All too often what an employee hears during the performance review is a surprise. Nothing the employee hears during this discussion should be a surprise. Any time something occurs throughout the year that deserves coaching and correction or praise and encouragement should be mentioned and addressed at the time it occurs. A performance review should be just that…a review…not a surprise.

- **Lack of Clarity of Expectations** – Very frequently organizations do a poor job of establishing performance expectations. When employees don't have clarity about expectations for their job, it is almost impossible to contribute what the organization and supervisors are expecting, yet they will be receiving a performance review documenting what they did or did not do well. No wonder employees look upon performance reviews with trepidation. Avoid this morale buster and ensure everyone can contribute effectively by ensuring every position has well-documented, shared, and thoroughly discussed performance expectations. A good process for ensuring employees have an opportunity to try to meet those expectations includes training, development, coaching, feedback, recognition and corrective action when needed.

- **Subjectivity** – In the absence of objective standards and expectations, supervisors have no option but to write performance reviews subjectively. By human nature, some subjectivity usually creeps into reviews, but favoritism and subjectivity can be minimized by writing performance reviews against well-established, openly shared expectations for each position. The more objective performance reviews are the more employees have the opportunity to excel, help the company meet expectations and truly enjoy their work.

History is hard to overcome and many, many employees and supervisors have negative experiences relating to performance reviews. As a leader, you have an obligation to simply not repeat history. Examine what is the state of performance reviews in your organization and commit to making more positive memories for yourself and your employees. You'll be rewarded with happier employees, the employees will have more job satisfaction, and overall the company will benefit. Take these steps to make performance review time a more effective, positive experience for all. Create a win/win/win for the leader, the employee and the organization.

My Story

I personally experienced the adverse impact of a poor performance review process. In my case, I had only one area that kept coming up as a "need to improve", but no one seemed to be able to give me any concrete examples of what I was doing wrong. It is much harder to improve when you don't know specifically what you should be working on, don't you think?

Why is it we put managers in positions of responsibility where they can impact both so many people and such a large portion of the company's results, yet we give them very poor training on how to be successful and help others?

I am so pleased I've been able to help others be better managers and supervisors. My hope is that the result ends up being more positive performance reviews, managed in an enriching and empowering manner rather than perpetuating dread and gloom.

Personal Branding

Much of personal success starts with creating and continually molding your personal brand. Your behaviors and results are the outward manifestation of your personal brand. Several years ago I developed a Cultural Framework model to help guide the cultural development of a client organization. I've adapted this model into a Personal Branding Process model. Let's diagnose the model so you can analyze your own brand.

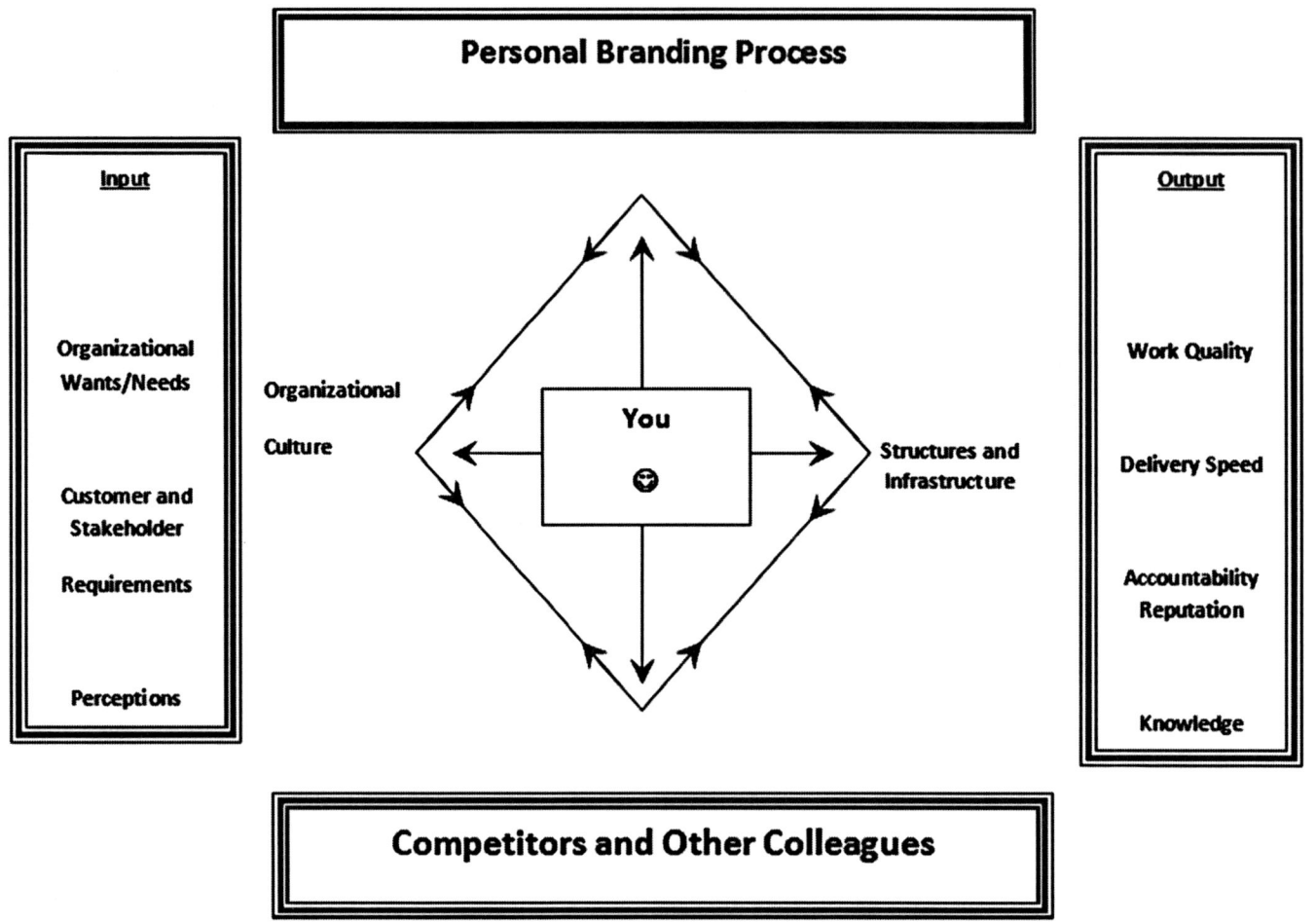

So how do you use this model to craft, shape or remake your own personal brand?

You are in the middle of the model. What causes you to behave as you do and, therefore, produce the results you deliver? The factors influencing your performance are made up of all of the items surrounding you…in the middle of the model.

Input examples are customer demands, things the boss is asking for, the needs of your team, your perception of the market, the norms and expectations of your organization, your personal history. Non-work Culture examples are your home environment, your heritage, your family values, your own beliefs based upon your experiences.

Competition examples are others vying for your job and interviewees for open positions or the competitive nature of the environment.

Organizational Culture and Structure examples are infrastructure and the 5 P's (policies, procedures, practices, processes and people).

Outputs examples are your work, results, behaviors, leadership, reputation, accountability, expertise, commitment and follow through.

All these forces factored together mold who you are, how you behave, how you go about your work, and the values you demonstrate in doing so. In short, the **Outputs** you produce and how you produce them.

Even in solopreneur (single person organizations) organizations all these forces are constantly in play. While in a larger organization there is more formality, nonetheless the entire model exists within a more casual, unwritten form in even the smallest organizations. This may sound academic, but that is not my intent. The intent is to give you a mechanism for analyzing what shapes your personal brand and a tool for analyzing and making adjustments.

Many years ago, I read a book entitled, *Lions Don't Need To Roar,* by Debra Benton. She writes about how the lion, because of personal branding…what she calls presence…. doesn't have to roar. The lion's brand alone establishes presence and reputation. To use a familiar phrase, their reputation precedes them. This model is offered as a way for you to do your own personal brand self-examination and be able to determine what, if anything, you need to adjust or develop further.

Why do you return to the same stores over and over again to buy the same products over and over again? Is it because of price, convenience, value, location, reliability, ambiance, friendliness, appearance or any of a number of other factors? So why do you think others continue to buy from you or seek you out? Is it the value you deliver, your appearance, your convenience or proximity to them, the ambiance you create, your friendliness or your price? Whether you are a business owner or an employee, all these questions apply equally. What you say, what you do, what you write, and how you do it are shaped by all the forces in the model and they converge to impact how you do your work and reflect your brand.

I challenge you to examine your personal brand and make it what it needs to be to enhance your success. If you don't consciously brand yourself, others will create a brand for you…and it may not be the brand you would prefer. Remember, the lion doesn't need to roar and neither do you.

My Story

It took me a while to get the meaning behind *Lions Don't Need to Roar.* Of course, lions need to roar I thought. How else do they attack, establish their presence, create dominance? Then I realized their personal brand was much more subtle even though they are the king of the jungle. Their silent swagger, size, huge mane, and physical presence brand them long before they ever need to roar. I got it. I gained new insight into the concept of personal branding.

So I began to examine my own brand. What did I want to project? What was I projecting? What presence did I convey? Was what I was conveying effective for my purpose? How did I need to change? What are the answers to these questions for you?

Planes, Trains, and Automobiles – Which is Best for Me?

"I just wanted to ask you, which way I ought to go?" "Well, that depends on where you want to get to," said the Cat. "It really doesn't matter..." said Alice. "Then it really doesn't matter which way you go," said the Cat...From <u>Alice's Adventures in Wonderland</u>

A movie and a fairy tale both point out the importance of having a plan. Just like <u>Alice in Wonderland</u> I can't tell you if a plane, a train or an automobile is best for you until you tell me where you want to go. If you want to get from here to there, you gotta have a plan.

<u>Where do YOU want to go? Where Do You Want To Take Your Business?</u>

I know as a business owner or manager you could describe to me what you want to achieve. I also know that if you have a business loan, you likely have prepared a financial plan for your banker. Great! You've had to think through your financial goals, your needs and how you plan to repay that loan.

This is a good start, but what about all the other aspects of your business? Finances are one very critical piece of business success, but they are only one piece and your financial goals will never be achieved if you don't also think about and plan for all the aspects of your business that support achieving financial success. What about your marketing plan? Sales plan? Employee development and satisfaction? Stakeholder satisfaction? All the entities in your supply chain? What about the internal processes necessary to produce your goods and services?

It is just amazing how many businesses do not have a comprehensive strategic plan and then they wonder someplace down the road why they aren't able to achieve their goals. They find themselves in an Alice in Wonderland-dilemma. (That's when they call me in a panic!) Much like Alice they often seek advise of which way to go, but haven't determined where "there" is or how they want to get there.

So what are the <u>benefits</u> of having a strategic plan?

Simply put a strategic plan:

➢ Guides the decisions you make along the way.

➢ Becomes your yardstick for measuring progress.

➢ Is a communications vehicle for gaining support and commitment from your banker, employees and all other stakeholders.

➢ Focuses your mind on your goals while facilitating informed choices along the way.

But wouldn't having a strategic plan mean I'll be limited and have to follow it strictly?

To the contrary, having a plan provides a good guide and like any guide you can deviate from it as needed as you move along toward your goal. Just like driving across the city, you think you'll take one route to your destination, but when you come upon a detour you deviate still keeping the destination in mind.

Do you have a strategic plan for your business? For your life? What's in it? Do you use it? Did you create it and put it in a drawer or on a shelf? Are you using it actively to guide your decisions toward your goals? Start now by writing down your goals and indicate how you can measure your progress toward them.

"I just wanted to ask you, which way I ought to go?" "Well, that depends on where you want to get to," said the Cat.

My Story

Children's stories offer so many valuable life principles. While we read them to children for the pure pleasure of spending time together, we are imparting valuable lessons at the same time. Every evening I am with my granddaughter when she is going to bed, we read together. Besides sharing our love she learns something and so do I.

I heard of another valuable use for children's books while speaking with a twenty-something friend this summer who had taught herself several languages. I asked her how she had learned to speak so many languages at such a young age. She said she buys children's books in her own native tongue (Swedish) and in the tongue of the language she wanted to learn. She uses the two to help her with learning the words and the grammar differences in each language. What a great idea. They are inexpensive, easy to carry with you as you learn, and effective. What have you learned from a children's book lately? After all, some would say we learned everything we really need to know by the time we go to kindergarten.

Service Performance Impact on Accountability

Here's the **situation**. We've been having our home remodeled. You know the drill. It's a mess to live through the process, but you do it for the new look, function and liveability of the space once it is finished. We've done this several times in our 45-year marriage so it is not a new experience for us. (Oh, please believe that I don't look that old!) This, however, is the first time I've been extremely frustrated with the service performance of the contractor. (I know what you're thinking if you've been through this experience too: I'm lucky it is the first time this has happened.)

Here's the **scenario**. The contractor says he'll be here at 9:30 and arrives at 11 meanwhile my life is on hold waiting for him to arrive. He says he'll work on Saturday, but doesn't call and doesn't come until Monday. He has had several situations that have caused legitimate delays (weather delaying cutting holes in the roof, automobile accident where he was at the wrong place at the wrong time), but he presents these situations as excuses rather than presenting how he will adjust and get the project on track. The saving grace is he is doing high quality work.

The **message** is why would you as a business owner sacrifice your reputation and future business referrals when delivering exceptional service is so easy? I'm delighted with the quality of his work and from that perspective am happy to recommend him to others. However, I'll have to tell anyone inquiring about his lack of accountability and service performance. This negative reflection could be avoided. It is so easy to pick up the phone and tell your client that due to uncontrollable circumstances (car accident, weather) you need to reschedule or will be late or that due to heavy rain you're not able to get the sky lights put in this week. However, you'd like to discuss how you might be able to make other adjustments to get back on track (work late, come earlier, work on the weekend, etc.). Nearly all of the time customers will be sympathetic and understanding. I know I would be. But when a call isn't made and the weather is used as a whiny excuse (and other work that is not weather dependent isn't done during this time frame), these multiple excuses soon begin to tarnish an otherwise good reputation.

When you own your own business (and even if you work for someone else) all you really ever have is your reputation and it can be controlled. We can't control getting caught in an auto accident that you didn't cause or the weather, but we can control our reaction to these circumstances and the impact they have on others.

This remodeling experience is a good reminder to me as a business owner. What are you doing to control your reaction to the unforeseen and its impact on the service performance and quality of delivery to your clients, customers and other stakeholders?

My Story

My father was an entrepreneur so I had the opportunity to see first-hand how important accountability is for a successful business. To me it is almost synonymous with integrity. In my view integrity is greatly diminished if you don't do what you say you are going to do. This is the basis of accountability. Dad often went above and beyond because he thought it was the right way to service his clients. I don't recall that he ever told me to be accountable, but his actions and my parents' expectation told me I had to be true to my word. Just another example of how important our actions are - others are learning and watching even if we don't know they are doing so.

Spending to Save

Sometimes you have to spend time, money, or resources up front in order to save in the long run. It's kind of like insurance. Every time I pay the house, car, life, health, and business insurance premiums I think of how much more disposable income I would have if I didn't make these payments. However, I know in the long run I am wiser and more prudent for making these payments. If you just have one real need for any of these types of coverage you are delighted you made those payments. I was raised with this philosophy as my father, whom I revered and respected tremendously, was a life insurance executive.

The same holds true for many of the good management practices we know we should practice, but often don't. Here are a few: Preparing well before conducting meetings, writing policies and procedures, following checklists, dedicating time to proper hiring and training, establishing and following communications methods to keep staff well informed, creating and following a strategic plan, and establishing objective and quantifiable measures.

Here is a valuable, thought-provoking way to look at preparing for and conducting meetings that is unique, but has some solid wisdom behind it. I credit Seth Godin, best-selling author of more than 12 books, for the essence of these ideas. His blog offers tips on how to ensure meetings are short, focused and productive which I have slightly added to. You can find Seth's complete text on his blog at http://sethgodin.typepad.com

➢ Plan ahead by ensuring you get the right people and only the right people in the room. The right people are primarily those that need to be there because they 1) have a vested interest in the topic and decisions being made and/or, 2) have information necessary to the decision. Don't waste the time and talent of others by unnecessarily inviting them to the meeting. If you or the attendees can't state why they are being included, they likely don't need to be there.

➢ Ensure meetings start on time and end when the end needs to occur, not when the calendar or conference room schedule says they should be ending. Give everyone the gift of time by ending early or give the organization the gift of a good discussion and decision if the meeting needs to go a bit longer. Timeliness honors and respects those who arrive on time. Become known as a person who starts on time and can be relied upon to manage a meeting efficiently and productively.

➢ Make sure you publish the purpose, desired outcomes and expectations before the meeting and then conduct the meeting toward these purposes.

➢ Set the stage as necessary – make introductions, make the environment welcoming and appropriate, and state the intended outcomes as you start the meeting.

➢ If equipment is needed, set everything up and ensure it is fully functioning before everyone arrives. This is not only efficient, it is a clear sign of respect for the time of others.

➢ Keep an Action Log. This is a simple document that records any action item that was assigned during the meeting. Send the Action Log to all attendees via an email following the meeting so everyone knows the outcomes, expectations and timelines for the next steps. This simple step exponentially increases the probability that action items will get done. And after all, isn't taking action why you called the meeting in the first place? The Action Log also serves as a review document for follow-up and completing outstanding items.

Frequently the best way to change an organization that may have fallen into sloppy habits is to simply start doing things differently. It isn't necessary to state that you're going to "run meetings differently around here". Just start running meetings differently. Pretty soon you'll have people noticing and appreciating the difference. This is one improvement you can do that costs you only a small bit of preparation time and gains you significant rewards in productivity, effectiveness, respect and in the long run saves money. The best leadership is by example so start today!

My Story

Toward the end of my corporate career I was on a world-wide leadership team installing a set of software functions through our corporation. I recall every Thursday afternoon having a 3-hour meeting with the rest of the global team. We were all on conference phones with the same set of data displayed on the large screen in our project War Room. It was always a grueling 3 hours and often ran over. It wasn't OK to not be there and it wasn't OK to leave early so you just endured. I often remember thinking I didn't need to be there for the entire 3 hours.

I had an important role and I wanted to keep others informed of my progress, needs and status. We devoted a lot of time on technical reporting that I couldn't contribute to nor could I take action on the information the technical group shared. I knew there was a better way of conducting meetings, but given that I was not a "techie" and this was definitely a technology-oriented group, I felt pretty powerless to influence the methods of our meetings.

To the group's credit we did use an action log. This was the first time I'd been engaged with a group that used one. It kept everyone informed, kept everyone accountable to one another, and was a great repository for gauging our progress and achievements.

Take Care of the Culture, Everything Else Will Follow

A few weeks ago Harvey MacKay wrote in his syndicated column about the idea that if you take care of the culture in your organization, everything else will follow. I couldn't agree more. Actually I believe this is true in any group of people whether it is a business, a family, a social club or a country.

Culture is similar to personality in that it is largely a subconscious collection of attitudes, beliefs and actions which influence individual behaviors and, therefore, results. So the culture of an organization becomes the collective beliefs, attitudes and actions of the employees. Organizational performance, therefore, is a direct result of the culture within an organization. Creating a robust, healthy, empowering culture where employees feel valued and appreciated for their contribution is a pretty powerful leadership imperative. Unfortunately, many people in leadership positions (I'm tempted to say most!) spend very little time thinking about or intentionally focusing on creating a culture that supports their intended goals.

There are many, many reasons for this, but I suspect one of the key reasons for not doing so is the fact that most companies don't tangibly measure and reward leaders for developing the "softer" side of their business. They are looking for a quick fix. But just like the stock market, investments in people and organizational capability are long-term propositions yielding benefits over time, not over night.

The fact is most managers get rewarded for meeting financial goals not for building an organization capable of reaching financial goals. But how are the employees supposed to be able to meet the financial goals if there is little overt attention paid to positively creating and supporting their skill and the overall organizational capability?

Frequently clients tell me what they wish for, what they think is wrong, what they are experiencing as undesirable results, but few take the time to determine the root cause. Here are a few examples of root causes which adversely impact both human and financial performance and, consequently, often adversely impact an organization's culture.

➢ High turnover costs are often rooted in poorly defined job expectations and weak hiring processes.

➢ Employees feeling they aren't listened to stems from weak management skills and few, if any, intentionally designed communication processes. Managers are likely talking and telling more than asking and listening.

➢ Work force members not knowing where the company is going is due to leadership not specifically defining and sharing company goals and failing to highlight the key role employees play in making these goals a reality.

➢ Favoritism emerges in the absence of objective standards of performance as a basis for performance evaluations and also as a basis for recognition and rewards.

➢ Questionable behaviors and ethical issues arise when companies don't have well-articulated values or when the values they have are platitudes rather than the bedrock for how the company is operated.

➢ Top performers become concerned when they can't see a career path and little attention is paid to succession planning.

While these are just a few of the more common examples, you get the idea. Almost any leadership issue that comes up is grounded in organizational culture. It all comes down to the **5 P's - People, Processes, Policies, Practices, and Procedures**. Examine these and you'll find the root cause of performance issues. (See also article entitled 5 P's of Organizational Leadership in this book.)

People – What are your hiring practices? Do you search for and select candidates based upon the competencies needed for the job? Are your interview questions crafted to find out how the candidates have performed in job-like situations in the past? How are employees evaluated, recognized and rewarded? Do people understand where the company is going, what the organizational goals are and how they help make those goals a reality? Do the employees understand WIIFT (What's in it for them)?

Processes – Are the step-by-step processes used in the operation of the organization well thought out? Could you truly draw a flow chart or the processes end-to-end ensuring there are no overlaps and gaps? If there are overlaps you have redundancy built in which sometimes is necessary as a fail-safe, but can also be a waste of labor and materials if taken too far. Gaps mean opportunities for errors and mistakes are built into the system. Gaps mean someplace along the line you aren't going to produce the service or product the customer is looking for. Oops!

Policies – Having too many policies defined too strictly can cause a stiff, uncaring, mechanical environment. Yet, it is critical to have the core few policies well defined, well thought through and shared with all employees. Everyone needs to understand the "rules of the game" if the game is going to be played in a collaborative, supportive, well-skilled organization.

Practices – Practices are those behaviors and expectations that happen in the work place, but that aren't written down. They are the unwritten, unspoken, but yet critically important norms of "how we do things around here".

Procedures – Procedures are the step-by-step definitions of how policies are implemented. They explain the tactical "how-to's" of how things get done. They are the check lists and explanations used to help train new employees and are used as a guide to ensure consistency and thoroughness on the more complex tasks performed in the organization.

So where are the gaps and/or overlaps in the 5 P's of your organization? Do you need to assess how well you are performing against the 5 P's? If you find inconsistent results, things not getting done and yet people feeling like they are doing their job thoroughly, people not knowing what or how to do their jobs, or a lack of commitment start by making an honest evaluation. As a result, you'll not only improve your organizational operating performance, you'll also strengthen your organizational culture.

My Story

In 1985, I was part of a small in-house consulting group who provided process and organizational improvement consulting to our external clients. We called our group Champions for Customer Success. It was a very descriptive and appropriate title because we provided our service gratis in the spirit that if we helped our clients and suppliers become more efficient, effective and profitable in the long run we would become more profitable also. It was a ground-breaking approach and definitely out-of-the-box for the time.

As a part of the work we did, we often analyzed the data we found from our client engagements to 1) better understand individual client needs, 2) refine our own processes and services and 3) determine if there were universal, common needs throughout each industry segment we serviced. I stumbled onto the 5 P's idea from this analysis. In the particular type of consulting I provided, the concerns always involved one or more of the 5 P's. This holds true in my private practice also.

Which if the 5 P's are working well in your organization? Which ones need attention? What is you action plan?

Tips for Managing in Tough Times

It is never easy to manage a business. There are always a multitude of people, product, process and service issues to be juggled and prioritized. Add to this mix the heightened pressures in today's business world and it is no wonder today's managers feel especially stressed. We've never been in a time when we all felt we had to do more with less and yet never has it been more important to satisfy both your employees and customers. How do you do all this when the limited resources at your disposal all seem to have become even more scarce? Here are some ideas for managing in today's tough times.

BITES – Belief, Intent, Target, Expectation, Share

<u>Belief</u> in your self and your staff - If you don't convey confidence through your own beliefs and actions, your staff cannot project confidence to your customers.

<u>Intent</u> – Be intentional in your actions and your words. If you've got a strategic plan, follow it, talk about it and reference it as you make your decisions; communicate the intent of your actions and decisions in alignment with your plan. Everyone can then see how your decisions and intentional actions move the entire organization closer to your goals. This is a fabulous way to lead by example. And by all means, if you don't have a strategic plan, create one – it is the best assurance you have for ending up where you want to be rather than some unintended place.

<u>Target</u> – Set realistic milestones aligned with your overall targeted goals. You achieve big goals by taking one intentional step at a time toward your targeted dreams.

<u>Expectations</u> – Expect success, expect results, expect a lot of yourself and expect a lot of others. Expectations set the tone for what we will or will not achieve. If we think we can, we can. If we think we can't, we won't.

<u>Share</u> - Achieving results and managing toward success starts with personal leadership. But to be effective and have the organization move forward dreams, goals and plans must be written down, talked about, and shared openly.

You eat a big block of Swiss cheese, one morsel at a time – enjoy all those tasty BITES.

BE FABB – Firm, Ask, Back, Bold

I got this from Sharon Lechter, author of *Three Feet From Gold* and several other best selling books (www.sharonlecter.com). You have to BE FABB because no one will hire you or buy your products or come to you for service if you aren't…

<u>Firm</u> – A firm handshake establishes confidence, takes trust to the next level of depth, and creates personal connection.

<u>Ask</u> – Asking questions causes you to listen more than talk and listening is the key to servicing, selling and satisfying others.

<u>Back</u> – A straight, erect back looking the other person in the eye with a purposeful, confident posture establishes your presence and is the first step toward instilling trust.

<u>Be Bold</u> – Being bold requires confidence, knowledge and a projection of capability – all key ingredients for business and personal success.

REMINDERS of things you know, but may have forgotten…that are so important in these times.

* Make a DO NOT DO list to ease your mind and gain valuable focus.

* Rejoice rather than worry – focus on your abundant blessings. Worry is praying for what you DON'T want.

* Quit trying to find the "one" right answer – focus on options and possibilities.

* Live your life for yourself rather than for others.

- RUN, DON'T WALK away from negative people – surround yourself with those who believe in possibilities.

- Hire slow, fire fast – get the right people on the bus and help those who are misplaced get off the bus.

My Story

As frequently as possible I attend the presentations offered by the National Bank of Arizona Women's Financial Group (WFG) (www.nbarizona.com/specialty-wfg). They often have authors and leading business people headline their events and their topics are always enlightening, thought-provoking and often inspiring. I got the ideas for BITES and BE FABB from Sharon Lechter's WFG presentation. Simple acronyms are easy to remember and these two offer such good advice. Thank you, Sharon and WFG.

Trends

What are the environmental factors in your region of the country? Are any of these factors indicating you should be shifting your focus or preparing for change? In our area we have been in a transition period for several years and this is true for much of the country. What are the economic, environmental, social and business implications of these trends for your business?

Like much of the south western US, the growing shift is away from a rural economy toward a knowledge-based economy. For Arizona, this means we have shifted away from the C's.

From	To
Cotton	Trade
Cattle	Tourism
Citrus	Globalization
Copper	Demographics
Climate	

Climate is the one constant as our perpetually sunny skies and spectacularly beautiful scenery sell easily to tourists. All other factors though have dramatically changed. And in some parts of the country even the weather patterns have changed. So what is the impact on you and your business due to the shifts happening in your part of the country?

As an Organizational Development Specialist, these shifts mean I need to be prepared to:

- Advise business owners and leaders on the impact of labor issues such as immigration and the changing attitudes of the generations?

- Facilitate strategy development regarding a shortage of skilled labor amidst high unemployment.

- Understand my clients are seldom "from here" but have moved into the Valley – they do not have deep roots.

- Help them face change management issues such as growth and technological infrastructure changes.

- Understand their concerns are not just about "off shore" trade, but also "near shore" trade as our economy has both a dramatic micro and macro effect.

- Simultaneously, identify new emerging leaders while addressing succession planning needs.

- Recognize that tourism is a mainstay in our area and as a sector the industry in general is often unwilling to or unaware of the need to get outside counsel on the host of organizational issues this industry faces.

- Constantly be aware of technical innovations and the application of technology for business purposes.

- Remember that an overriding factor in almost all businesses in the Southwest is the fact that this region of the country is generally not a headquarters location. We have some regional headquarters, but very few corporate headquarters so the top decision makers are almost always in some other place.

- Keep in mind the impact of long-term sustainability concerns which none of us individually, but all of us collectively, can solve such as water, air, and infrastructure issues.

These are just a few of the impacts of trends in our region. As you look ahead the next two to three years, what are the shifts you have to anticipate for your profession, industry and region? What do you need to be doing now to be prepared? What counsel or outside expertise should you be considering?

My Story

I am in the midst of helping an organization develop a succession planning process. One of their seasoned, very wise leaders just this week said they thought they would be remiss if they concentrated on just the key success factors needed to excel in each of the leadership positions. Others were surprised by this comment as they were thinking it was critical to identify the core factors needed to excel. Well, they are both right.

You do need to have the core success factors well in hand, but the seasoned, wise leader is also correct. Her point was that she felt they had too often had myopic vision and the successful leaders of the future for their organization needed to have wider peripheral vision about other factors impacting their clients and the needs of their organization. She is so right. Her broader peripheral vision is one of the aspects of her character that makes her one of their wiser leaders. So what do you need to have in your peripheral vision? Is your leadership too myopic?

Using Mental Models as Decision Making Tools

Thinking in pictures, seeing circumstances as a series of cause and effects, and using theoretical models or mental models as guides for making decisions comes natural to about 50% of the population. To 50% of the population seeing things in this perspective feels foreign and may even feel like work. It isn't a matter of intelligence or education. It is a matter of natural preference for how we see the world. However, for all of us learning to see and use mental models as decision-making aids can be very beneficial.

Simple 2 X 2 matrices are easy to remember, can represent a wide variety of situations in a simple format, and can help sort out complex situations and reduce them to a manageable few set of circumstances upon which to base your decision.

One I have recently developed is a great tool for sorting out the impact any employee has on the performance and culture of an organization. I call it a Cultural Performance Matrix. It is particularly useful in sorting out the importance of a manager's or supervisor's performance versus their impact on the culture of the organization.

If you believe as I do that the more a manager or leader understands the importance and visibility of their role in shaping both the organizational culture and results, the more valuable this model becomes as a tool for decision making. Here is the model…

Cultural Performance Matrix

A Decision Matrix for Managing Performance and Shaping Organizational Culture

PERFORMANCE	Low Impact on Culture	High Impact on Culture
High	Positive Potentials Performing, but not Maximizing Potential Value	Superstars Leaders Early Adopters Influencers of Others
Low	Fence Sitters Will either become a Superstar or a Loser	Losers Corrective Action and/or Termination Needed

Impact on Culture

So how do you read the matrix and how do you use it to make effective decisions?

Losers – You all know who these employees are. They are the ones infecting everyone else with negative attitudes, rumor and innuendo, etc. You can't afford to have them infect others and undermine the performance-based culture you are trying to foster. They are carriers of these infectious diseases. These employees don't get it. They don't understand the culture you are trying to create nor are they performing. They are the ones you've tried to train and motivate but they just don't respond. Get your documentation in order and terminate them before they infect more good performers.

Positive Potentials –These are the folks that frustrate you, but don't necessarily consume your time the way Losers do. They are producing, but you know they could be doing more to help, you believe they have more capability and capacity, but because they generally don't cause trouble you just leave them alone. After all, your time is consumed by managing the behavior of the Losers.

Fence Sitters – These employees are contributors and they behave according to the organization's cultural values, but they just get by. Nothing is really wrong but you know they could be doing more. Corrective action and coaching may get them to step up to the challenge and become real leaders. Try to get them into situations where they are influenced more by the Super Stars than by the Losers. Protecting this group is one big reason for moving the Losers out of the culture as quickly and painlessly as possible.

Superstars – Their name describes their behavior and value. They understand what is expected and why it is important, they are leaders, they are high producers, and they positively influence the behavior of others. These are the real keepers. They are early adopters and the leaders who help move your organization forward toward your goals.

Very frequently I run into situations where managers know an employee is in the Fence Sitter or Loser category, but they haven't documented the employee's performance or talked with the employee. When I ask them why, they often say, "because it is so hard to hire good employees that I can't afford to lose them".

My position is that it is better to have fewer employees who are either Positive Potentials or Superstars than to deal with the "carrying costs" of managing the poor performers. You know how much time you spend trying to manage the behavior and performance of these few when your effort would be so much more enjoyable, rewarding and productive if it were spent helping and developing the majority who really produce and help you achieve your goals. It's the 80/20 rule, but we get caught up in spending 80% of our time on the wrong group of employees.

My Story

This particular 2 X 2 came out of an experience I had with a small specialty manufacturer of precision equipment. The company has about 75 employees many of whom are long-term. And as in many small companies, little training and development is provided. I was engaged to design and facilitate a supervisory training program. This simple format helped the shop-floor managers categorize the performance of each individual and determine how to best help each person. Then they were able to integrate their training objectives into performance objectives for the coming year. Without an easy to use, common language format for all to refer to, this group of managers simply saw the employees as a mass of 75 people. Now they had a way of differentiating and developing in a more targeted, focused manner.

About the Author

Joyce A. Friel is the president of Peak Performance Consulting, LLC, an organizational development consultancy focusing on assessment and design of organizational and business solutions that deliver results.

Friel serves as a business leader, strategist, facilitator, catalyst and developer. Her experience comes from having led change in both Fortune 500 companies and smaller organizations for more than 30 years. She has been successfully helping clients grow their businesses as a private consultant since founding Peak Performance Consulting in 2001.

Her enthusiasm and commitment for building capability in organizations is evident in the energy and conviction she brings to her work and she knows how to apply her experience in a hands-on, practical, results-oriented manner. She is passionately dedicated to the value received from focusing on the "soft stuff" which leads to an improved "hard stuff" bottom line.

Friel is a certified Senior Professional in Human Resources (SPHR) and has an undergraduate degree from University of Indianapolis and a master's degree in management with honors from Regis University; she has completed advanced work at Colorado State University and Columbia University.

She is a contributing author to *Six Sigma: The First Ninety Days* published by Prentice-Hall in 2006 and is a guest writer for "Ask the Experts" column of *The Arizona Republic*.

CPSIA information can be obtained at www.ICGtesting.com
Printed in the USA
BVOW05s1749200813

329080BV00015B/596/P

9 781466 438354